Advantage Contractor
Business Success Series

Volume 9:
Lien Law for Construction Contractors

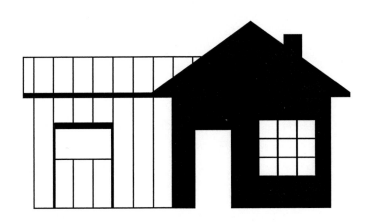

Gene Fessenbecker

About the Construction Contracting Academy

The Academy was founded in 1991 by Gene Fessenbecker to provide materials any independent contractor could use to start a contracting business correctly or to improve one that was operating. Shortly thereafter, the Oregon Legislature adopted a law requiring new contractors in Oregon to take 16 hours of education in "Laws and Business Practices Affecting Contractors." Gene took his information and set up the first written home study courses on the business of construction contracting. These courses were accredited by the Oregon Construction Contractors Board and still set the standard by which this type of course is judged.

Now these courses and others are available to all those people who want to do their trade as a business, as well as those who want to set up a contracting firm and hire trades people. The courses offered by the Academy through this Series allow you to start and operate a contracting business with more comfort by reducing the risk you face. Through the study of these courses and implementation of the routines and practices you can rise above the average and achieve business success in construction contracting.

Publisher's Cataloging-in-Publication
(Provided by Quality Books, Inc.)

Fessenbecker, Gene.
    Advantage Contractor Business Success Series / Gene
Fessenbecker. -- 1st ed.
    v. cm.
    Includes bibliographical references and index.
    Preassigned LCCN: 97-070190
    ISBN: 1-888198-24-9

    1. Construction industry--Management--United States.
I. Title. II. Title: Advantage Contractor Business Success
Series

HD9715.U6F47 1998   338.4769'068
                QBI98-451

Published by **Construction Contracting Press**,
a division of the CONSTRUCTION CONTRACTING ACADEMY
83 Centennial Loop • Eugene, Oregon 97401 • (541) 344-1442 •
1-800-937-2242 • (541) 344-5387 Fax   www.Contracting-Academy.com

Advantage Contractor Business Success Series

About the Author

Gene Fessenbecker, author and President of the Construction Contracting Academy, has done remodeling, custom home building, restoration and repairs as a general contractor, and worked as manager and operator of four different construction businesses over a period of 20 years. Gene wrote thirteen accredited self-study courses for the Oregon Contractors Prerequisite Education Program which have been offered through the Construction Contracting Academy since 1992. Currently, in addition to writing about the business of construction contracting, he is a dispute settler for home owner and home inspection warranty programs. Gene lives in Eugene, OR in a house that he has remodeled twice in the last 16 years.

Doing Your Part in Using this Book

We have done our best to provide useful and accurate information in this book. Every precaution has been taken to give you a product that you can use to build a productive contracting business. You have to take the information and use it as presented and do the work of operating a business, as described, to gain the best results. However, neither the publisher nor the author assumes any liability for damages incurred through the use of this book.

Special Thanks

The Advantage Contractor Business Success Series is a product of many special people. At the beginning of the Oregon Contractor Education Program Joe DeMarzo was instrumental in getting courses into finished condition. Laura Stine took many organizational and personnel challenges and found solutions. Don Sirkin provided financing to the fledgling company. Linda Seaman and Liz Overstreet made many changes to stabilize the growing business. Later all of these efforts are brought to bear on this Series. Angela Lewis and Linda Seaman made the difference as the new courses grew into being. Thanks to these and all the others who had a hand in the success of the Academy.

Contents

Chapter 4: Alternatives to Lien Action

Quick Reference Tool

You, Our Customer

Small Business Help

Resources

Bibliography

Web Sites

Index

Table of Figures

About This Series

For most people who go into it, construction contracting is a way of practicing a construction trade. For others it can be a means of doing business. The *Advantage Contractor Business Success Series* is designed mainly for tradespeople who are running a contracting business. However, even seasoned business people can benefit from the information in this course.

"There is only one success-to be able to spend life in your own way."
Christopher Morley

Contractor business records from around the country show that fewer than one in five firms survive the first five years of business. Nationwide an average of 20 percent of new contractors are not in business at the end of the first year.

Going into any business is risky. Most businesses that fail do not return the initial amount invested. One of the main benefits in starting a contracting business seems to be the low start-up costs. Perhaps the ease of getting started, and the lower apparent risk, brings people into contracting who are not prepared to stay in business. The *Advantage Contractor Business Success Series* came about to fill this lack of business skill among contractors.

Rules of Business

Many individuals do succeed in the contracting business. The Academy believes successful contractors have learned the rules of business and follow them every day.

The rules of business exist to serve us. Often business rules have to be adapted carefully to a specific business to be of the most use. Therefore, the goal of this series of courses is to put these rules in your hands, like your trade tools, so you can use them effectively.

All I ask is an honest advantage.

Rules of Business as Tools of Business

All tools have to be ready to use and in good condition to be useful, whether they are for trade or for business. In addition, one has to know how to use the tools well. Knowing where the tools are is only part of the solution. Using any tool skillfully takes instruction and practice.

Most of you have worked hard to learn your trade. Now you can enjoy applying the skills of your trade and take pride in your work.

The skills of operating a business are strange and different for most new contractors. It takes time and effort to learn your business skills as well as you have learned your trade. However, as a contractor, you need these business skills as much as your trade skills.

The Academy has combined information from a number of business professionals with the knowledge of contracting. We know first hand what construction contracting is about.

Money Making Tools for Your Business Workbelt℠

The information acquired from the *Advantage Contractor Business Success Series* allows you to keep improving your business skills.

New information has to be worked into your routines to be useful. You will have to make room for the new, more useful information while you discard the old. This is similar to taking an old, worn out tool from your workbelt and replacing it with a new, more useful tool.

To keep improving your contracting business, you will want to keep the most useful and up-to-date tools in your business workbelt. To do this, you can take advantage of the 30 years of contracting and business experience I bring to this course. The successful use of business tools is critical to a new contractor. I can help you with your business right away by giving you specific information you can put to use today.

Self-Paced Personal Instruction

One of the easiest ways to learn as a part-time student is through a home-study course. You study when you have some extra time and where you can be most comfortable.

For an adult, self-paced personal instruction usually offers the most useful educational experience. You can set your own pace, your own time to study, and the amount of effort you want to put into the material. In this way you receive the greatest personal benefit for the time you spend.

> "I am convinced that it is of primordial importance to learn more every year than the year before. After all, what is education but a process by which a person begins to learn how to learn."
> Peter Ustinov

> "Success is merely a matter of luck. Ask any failure."
> Earl Wilson

About This Course

Discussion is an exchange of knowledge. Argument is an exchange of ignorance.

The Construction Contracting Academy welcomes the opportunity to provide you with the *Advantage Contractor Business Success Series* course, *Lien Law for Construction Contractors*.

This course is one in the *Adavantage Contractor Business Success Series*. A complete list of all the courses available through the Construction Contracting Academy is available at the beginning of this course.

A *lien* is a legal right to have property sold or its value applied to the payment of a claim. Lien law can be a major benefit to a contractor when there is a dispute about payment for work done to a property. This law keeps an owner from receiving a benefit from a contractor and not paying for that benefit. The contractor can use the lien law to collect for work performed.

Purpose

The purpose of this course is to provide you, the contractor or subcontractor, with information necessary to protect and enforce your right to a lien. In addition, you are exposed to the specific laws that regulate your activities as a contractor.

Your best strategy as a general contractor or subcontractor is to select and practice using all the correct and useful business and legal tools you can find.

Benefits to You

As a general contractor or subcontractor on a construction project, you will benefit by complying with the lien law statutes of your state. These statutory requirements may seem rigid, but are in fact designed to strike a balance between the rights of claimants and the rights of interest holders (owners).

You will increase your general knowledge about securing payment for lienable performance through the construction lien law process. This course will enable you to evaluate your own business practices to discern whether they protect and enforce your right to a lien.

Organization of the Course

This course consists of this introduction and five chapters that:

- Introduce the lien law statutes and categories of lienable performance.
- Examine underlying contractual issues important in a lien law case.
- Review the statutory notice forms and requirements necessary to protect and enforce a lien.
- Consider alternatives to the lien law process for resolving disputes and/or securing payment.
- Provide definitions of useful terms specific to lien law.

This will present you with options and show you how other factors may affect your right to a lien.

Chapter 1: Lien Law Simplified

This chapter covers:

- Definitions of some statutory terms used throughout the course
- Categories of lienable performance
- Principles of construction lien law

Chapter 2: Contractual Issues

This chapter discusses various aspects of construction contracts that affect a contractor's lien rights such as:

- Proper and substantial contract performance
- Contract terms that limit, modify, or waive lien rights
- The determination of the amount of the lien
- The effect of claimant's breach of contractual obligations on the right to lien
- Alternatives for contract recovery

An ounce of facts is worth more than a ton of justification.

Chapter 3: Statutory Notice Forms and Requirements

This chapter covers the statutory notice forms and requirements under the statutes including:

- Delivery, response procedures and timelines
- Consequences of noncompliance
- Mandatory language.

It concludes with a step-by-step summary of both the claimant's and the owner's procedures.

Chapter 4: Alternatives to Lien Action

This chapter provides alternatives to the lien law process including:

- Ways to prevent a dispute, i.e., by defining specific performance in a contract and/or by developing useful communication techniques
- Other ways to secure payment for performance, i.e., suing the contractor's bond, filing a claim with the licensing or registration agency, or submitting a dispute to an arbitration or mediation organization for resolution

Those who don't read have no advantage over those who can't read.

Quick Reference Tool

The "Quick Reference Tool" at the end of the manual can be compared to a glossary because it defines and explains words and terms mentioned in the text.

Tip

Like most legal subjects, lien law uses many terms that are either unfamiliar to the average person or used in a specific legal manner.

For this reason, we strongly recommend that you read through the "Quick Reference Tool" before reading the rest of the manual.

You, Our Customer

As our customer, we are happy to demonstrate our customer service to you. As with all our courses, we at the Academy offer our services to you through these courses. If you have questions or problems, we would be happy to talk to you.

State Offices that Provide Small Business Help

You will find a list of states that have services to assist small businesses.

Resources

Here you will find sources of extra information on each part of the course. Many associations and groups offer information and programs to help your contracting business.

Bibliography

As a contractor you will always have an advantage if you keep studying and learning how to improve the operation of your business. These books can make a difference.

Web Sites

This section of the course will show you where to go on the net for the information you need.

Index

Chapter 1

Lien Law Simplified

Many an argument is sound, and only sound.

This chapter begins with a discussion of the development of lien law statutes and the legal terms used in them and throughout this course. It identifies the kinds of construction liens, explains lienable performance, lists the categories of lienable performance, and outlines each. Finally, it explains the significant principles of construction lien law.

Lien Laws

All lien laws are passed by state legislatures. There is no federal lien law. When any government agency files liens for taxes and other purposes, they must use the same state courts you would. In the District of Columbia the lien is filed with the Recorder of Deeds.

For the purposes of this course, it is assumed that there is a contract made with an owner of the real property which gives the contractor the right to claim a lien. This contract has to have been for services or improvements to the property of the owner. For questions about contract law please refer to the *Advantage Contractor Business Success Series* course, *Contract Law for Construction Contractors*.

Definition of Construction Lien

A lien is the legal right of a person to have property sold or its value applied to the payment of a claim for services to, delivery of products installed on, or improvements to, real property when the owner refuses to or cannot pay amounts due under a contract.

To review briefly, a *lien* is a legal right to have property sold or its value applied to the payment of a claim.

Lien Statutes or Laws

Statutes are laws or rulings made by a legislative branch of government and expressed in a formal document.

The statutes that pertain to the construction industry are contained in the state law section covering liens in general. The statutes that pertain to construction lien law in particular are contained in that part of lien law statutes that covers construction liens. Your state statutes will often make references to contract law, lien law, and contractor licensing or registration law, indicating that each section of the law will help clarify how they work together and how they are affected by each other.

No law has ever been passed that will keep a person from acting like a fool.

Warning
Construction liens are governed by these statutes and can be created and perfected only if the regulations as set forth in the statutes are strictly adhered to.

Construction lien statutes were first enacted in the eastern regions of the United States during the period of expansion and development that followed the American Revolution. These statutes were later introduced to the northwest regions in the second half of the nineteenth century when development in that area made construction lien statutes necessary.

Construction lien statutes were developed for two reasons:

- It is believed that construction lien statutes stimulate construction activity by assisting builders and suppliers in securing payment for performance.
- Because performance devoted to improving real property typically enhances the value of that property, it is only fair that the cost of performance be treated as a charge on the property.

Note
Before 1975, construction liens were termed "mechanic's and materialmen's lien. "Many states have made the change in terminology to reflect the fact that a lien is available to persons who are neither mechanics nor materialmen, such as architects, equipment rental dealers, and trustees of employee benefit plans.

StatuteTerminology
State statutes assign specific definitions to various legal terms. Contractors may be unfamiliar with these legal terms. Some of these

terms, which will be used throughout this course, include:

- Improvement
- Commencement of improvement
- Contractor
- Original contractor
- Subcontractor
- Owner
- Interest holders

Other terms found in the statutes and construction lien law appear in this manual. These are defined throughout the text and in the "Quick Reference Tool" of this course.

In most states, construction liens are part of a state's statutes on mechanic's liens. The law covers all cases where a person improved property and is then given the right to attach or sell the property to recover payment for work done. Lien law is a unique and powerful means for people doing trade work to recover payment.

Improvement

The term *improvement* refers to all of or a part of the construction project. The statutes liberally define *improvement* as "any building, wharf, bridge, ditch, flume, reservoir, well, tunnel, fence, street, sidewalk, machinery . . . and all other [applicable] structures or superstructures."

A house is an improvement. If the project consists of new construction then you would be constructing an improvement on the property. If the project is a remodel then the improvement is the work being done on the existing structure. Painting, roofing, and even cleaning can be improvements under the law.

Commencement of Improvement

Commencement of improvement is the first actual preparation or construction on the site, or the first delivery to the site of substantial materials.

The person who never makes mistakes must get awfully tired of doing nothing.

Contractor

Basically, the word *contractor* is defined as you would expect. It is a person who contracts to do all or part of the work and retains control of means, method, and manner of accomplishing the work. A contractor can provide just labor at the site, or materials, supplies, and labor at the site.

> ***Note***
> A construction lien can cover any labor, materials, supplies, services, and/or equipment used in a construction project, providing all other statutory criteria are met.

Original Contractor

Most state lien laws define *original contractor* as a contractor who has a contractual relationship with the owner. Commonly, the general contractor of a construction project is the only one who has a direct contract with the owner. General contractors, as such, are *original contractors*.

In contract law, the original contractor can also be referred to as the primary contractor. The contract between the owner and original contractor is referred to as the primary contract.

Ignorance of the law is an excuse for not being willing to learn enough to use the law for your benefit.

> ***Note***
> This manual uses either *original* or *general contractor* to refer to a contractor who has a direct contract with the owner.

Subcontractors

Subcontractors are not original contractors because they do not have a contract directly with the owner.

Most often only one original (general) contractor exists for a construction project. All other contractors working on the project are classified as subcontractors.

However, an owner will sometimes act as their own general contractor and will contract directly with subcontractors. In this situation, a subcontractor would then become an original contractor.

Subcontractors have lien rights, but must notify owners of their right to lien. Work with your general contractors to assist them in getting owners to accept and understand how liens work. More and more owners are aware of liens, but do not understand how they work.

Owner

Three types of owners are usually defined in lien law statutes:

- A person who is, or claims to be, the owner of the land or a portion of the land on which preparation or construction is performed

- A person who entered into a contract for the purchase of an interest in the land or improvement being charged with a lien
- A person who has a valid existing lease (lessee) on land or an improvement and who, on the basis of that lease, possesses an interest in the land or improvement

Tip
More than one owner can be involved in a construction project even though they did not sign a contract.

Interest Holders

Interest holders are those who share ownership of the property and/or improvements with the owner. This would include:

- Absentee owners
- Lessees
- Mortgagees (loan institutions or individual lenders)

Tip
Although loan institutions (mortgagees) are not considered owners under most state laws, it is wise to treat lenders as if they are owners. This is especially true when it comes to giving any type of lien notice regarding materials supplied for a project.

Filing and perfecting liens is mostly a matter of timing. The form is necessary, but filing on time is critical.

The construction lien statutes are designed to protect the rights of parties who hold an interest in the property and therefore will be affected by the lien. It often happens that these interest holders are not a party to the contract under which work and materials are furnished.

Note
The law attempts to strike a balance between the lien claimant's security and the property rights of interest holders. In fact, much of the complexity and procedural requirements of the law result from this quest for balance.

Construction Liens

A construction lien is a legal right to force a property to be sold to satisfy an unpaid claim. When a contractor is not paid for performing duties under the terms of a valid contract, a lien claim or suit can be filed against the property which was improved.

A construction lien does not attach to all types of property. It usually cannot attach to public property. In these cases there are other statutes designed to secure payment for performance devoted to the improvement of public property. These statutes are concerned with bond issues and are beyond the scope of this course. In brief, the contractor has to file suit to recover under the payment bond assigned to the project.

Seek to be reasonable in avoiding disputes. Be aware of the problems the other parties to a project might be having, it can only work to your benefit.

Lien on Privately-owned Property

The construction lien is a legal right to hold property or to have it sold or applied for payment of a claim. This legal right is granted by the statutes to persons who provide labor, materials, or certain services that are incorporated into, consumed in, or contributed to the improvement of privately owned real property.

A lien placed on the owner's interest (share) in the property is an encumbrance (liability) that remains in effect until the issue of payment is settled.

Again, the right to lien is a statutory right; it is not created by a contractual agreement. However, the right to lien assumes a contractual agreement exists.

Warning
Only those persons who have provided lienable performance at the request of the owner, or someone with authority to act for the owner, have a right to lien.

Lien on Commercial Property

A commercial improvement is any structure or building not used or intended to be used as a residential building, or other improvements to a site on which such a structure or building is to be located.

The lien law statutes for commercial property differ somewhat from those for residential property. The differences are noted wherever they apply throughout the course.

You will often be asked to provide a waiver of supplier or subcontractor lien rights. This is fine; but do not give away your own lien rights over to an owner until you are paid in full.

Lienable Performance in Construction

Lienable performance refers to any work, materials, equipment, and/or services provided for a construction project.

Qualification of Lienable Performance

Any assertions made about lienable performance have to be qualified. Mere performance does not create lien rights unless other factors are also present.

For example, the claimant will have to prove that the performance rendered was at the request of the owner or the owner's agent. Other issues include:

To prove loss in addition to basic labor and materials, you will have to show detailed records. What loss did you suffer and how does the contract grant you compensation?

- Quality of the performance
- How much (extent) of the property is subject to the lien; the lien could attach to the land, the improvement, or both
- Dollar amount of the lien
- Matters of perfection and priority

Providing lienable performance is only one of many steps in the process of enforcing a lien on the property. Other significant factors are discussed in Chapter 2: "Contractual Issues," and in Chapter 3: "Statutory Notice Forms and Requirements."

Categories of Lienable Performance

For a performance to be lienable it has to fall within specific categories as defined by state statute:

- Labor furnished for an improvement
- Materials furnished for an improvement (including transportation of materials)

- Equipment rental
- Contribution to an employee benefit fund
- Plans, drawings, specifications, and supervision
- Site preparation or development

Generally speaking, these categories define eligibility based on the nature of the work, not on the professional status of the claimant.

Although there are several categories of lienable performance, a claimant does not file separate claims for each category. For example, a claimant who has supplied both materials and labor for a project would file just one lien claim for that project that equaled the value of the total performance given.

A required mediation clause in your contract moves the dispute resolution up to the front of the project instead of the end.

Note

Persons eligible to file a lien claim are clearly defined under your state's lien law statutes.

Without exception, the courts have refused to expand the scope of the statutes to include claimants who do not clearly fall within the designated categories of lienable performance.

Lien for Labor on an Improvement

A lien for labor is available to general contractors or subcontractors who provide such performance for the construction of an improvement on real property.

If the contractors employ laborers, the lien may also be available to the laborers themselves for the amount of their wages or for the reasonable cost of their labor. The laborer may be any of the following:

- An employee of the owner
- An employee of the general contractor
- An employee of the subcontractor
- An independent party under contract with the general contractor or subcontractor

Note

Even though a laborer's lien is derived from a contract between the owner and the contractor, the lien is independent of that contractor. Therefore, even if the contractor breached the contract with the owner of the property, the laborer may still be entitled to a lien for the value of the total performance.

In a situation where a lien is claimed by the employer of laborers, it includes not only wages for labor but may also include:

- Travel and subsistence expenses
- Contributions paid by the employer to an employee benefit plan
- Overhead expenses allocated to the work performed
- Reasonable profit on work performed

Although the word *labor* is used in the statutes, the lien is not confined to manual labor. It covers supervision as well as all the other types of work or services, such as:

- Equipment operators
- Off-site fabrication
- Labor for adjustments

Labor also includes supervision and other work or services involved in the process of construction. For example, if an operator is furnished with rental equipment, a right to lien for the value of the operator's labor is created.

*Part of the business of contracting is telling owners about your lien rights; they should know. In many states the owner **must** be told. Make a point to be businesslike in how you deal with this.*

Labor for off-site fabrication is also lienable if all of the following conditions are met:

- Materials were ordered by the owner, contractor, or subcontractor for a particular project
- Fabrication was built to order in accordance with specifications
- Fabrication was ultimately incorporated into the improvement

Under certain circumstances, material suppliers may qualify for a labor lien. For example, if the material supplier performs extensive adjustments or corrective work in the course of incorporating the material into the structure, he or she would be eligible for a labor lien. This is true provided that the work needed was not due solely to defects in the material that were the fault of the supplier.

> ### *Note*
> Labor performed on a construction site will only be lienable if it relates directly to the improvement. For example, labor furnished for incidentals, such as the repair of construction equipment, is not lienable.

Lien for Materials

A lien for materials includes the cost of the tangible materials provided at the request of the owner or the owner's agent. It does not include the:

- Extension of credit for the purpose of acquiring the material
- Labor for production of the material
- Cost of transporting the material by the supplier

> ### *Note*
> The general contractor or subcontractor may file a lien for materials intended for construction which were purchased on credit but not yet paid for. The claimant does not have to prove materials have been paid for.
>
> The general contractor's or subcontractor's lien is effective until a lien is filed and foreclosed on by the supplier.

To qualify for a lien for materials, the following conditions usually have to be satisfied:

- Material has to be supplied with the intention of using it in construction on a specified project.
- Material has to be actually delivered to the site. It is not necessary that the claimant makes the delivery.
- Material has to be furnished for incorporation into or consumption in the erection of the structure.
- Materials have to be consumed, used up, or rendered valueless or unusable in the construction process. Tools or appliances that can be used again at the end of a project have not been consumed and therefore are not lienable.

Lawyers would have a hard time making a living if people behaved themselves and kept their promises.

Warning
If material was not supplied in reference to a specific project, it will usually be considered a sale of personal property and the seller has no lien rights, even if the material is incorporated into the structure. Invoices and receipts have to show the project site address or some other means of reference.

If the goal of filing a lien is revenge, the result can only be a bad deal.

Lien for Transportation of Materials

Transportation of materials is lienable as off-site labor when materials are transported by someone other than the supplier because the haul is closely related to construction.

Note
Hauling charges for materials delivered by the supplier are lienable as part of the cost of the materials.

Lien for Equipment Rental

In most states, the rental lien is subject to a limitation that does not apply to any other lien. The rental dealer is entitled only to a lien for reasonable rental value, even if the claimant has contracted directly with the owner at a higher rate.

Note
The lien for rental equipment covers rent due for the equipment. This is an exception to the general rule stating that where the claimant has a contract with the owner, the lien covers the contract price of labor and/or materials.

Lien for Contribution to an Employee Benefit Fund

The lien for contribution to an employee benefit fund is the only lien granted to a person (trustee of the employee(s)) who is not directly involved in the construction.

When contributions to a benefit fund are required on behalf of laborers who performed labor on an improvement, the fund itself will acquire a lien on the improvement for the amount of the contributions due for work performed.

Lien for Plans, Drawings, Specifications, and Supervision

In most states, the lien for plans, drawings, specifications, and supervision is confined to four professional classes:

- Architect
- Land surveyor
- Landscape architect
- Registered engineer

It is not clear, in most states, whether persons who provide services outside of these professional classes, a designer for example, would be entitled to a labor lien for work performed. It is reasonable to assume that the designer would be entitled to a labor lien for contributions to an improvement.

Architects and other professionals normally set up contracts to clear themselves of liability once the plans and specifications are accepted. The contractor is usually the liable party when a design or a specified detail is rejected or changed by building officials. Your best bet is to settle all liability issues on design prior to accepting a contract.

The lien for architectural and engineering services attaches the structure as well as the land affected by the plans or services provided. The statute permits a lien on the land and the structure, even if the planning or initial work does not result in the planned improvement.

Because a lien for this type of performance attaches to the land, the agreement for services has to be created by the professional and the owner or owner's conventional agent and not by the construction agent. The construction agent has the power to bind the owner for an improvement lien, but not for a land preparation lien.

Note
If the property is an owner-occupied residence, a direct contract with the owner is generally required. A lien is not usually permitted where the services were requested by the agent of the owner without a direct contract.

Learn how to disagree with people without being crazy, rude, crude or silly.

Lien for Site Preparation or Development
A lien on the land itself is permitted for labor, materials, and services that were furnished for the preparation or development of the land itself or of a neighboring street or road.

The distinction between work in preparing the land and work on an improvement on land is not easy to make. Generally, a lien for preparing the land is confined to work on the land that is intended to increase the land's value or utility for construction purposes at a present or future date.

> ### *Note*
> Site preparation is usually defined in these types of words "... excavating, surveying, landscaping, demolition and detachment of existing structures, leveling, filling in, and other preparation of land for construction." Therefore, enhancing the land for other purposes, for example farming, will not be lienable.

Legal Principles in Construction Lien Law

If you must argue, the best way to win is to start out by being right.

Filing a construction lien is the legal right of a person performing work on a qualified property who does not receive payment for that work. As with all legal processes, there are principles that apply specifically to lien law.

Principles of construction lien law are the rules of law that apply to construction liens. These principles act to define procedure and process in completing a successful construction lien.

Performance

Performance means that a contractor has done what was promised in the contract. This performance may be of any described part of the contract that directly and measurably improved a qualified property. Only that performance not compensated for may be claimed in a lien.

Agency

In a lien law case the creation of agency, as well as the terms and extent of the agency, has to be determined. Agency exists when an owner authorizes another to act on his or her behalf. This person who acts on behalf of the owner is called the owner's agent. There are two types of agency:

- Conventional
- Statutory (construction)

Conventional Agency

In a conventional agency, the agent has the authority to make contracts on the owner's behalf. This kind of agency grants the agent the power to bind the owner personally in other contractual agreements as well as to bind the property and/or improvement with a lien.

Conventional agency has three basic characteristics:

- Mutual consent between the owner and agent exists to have this relationship.
- Proof exists that the conventional agent and the owner agreed to the relationship.
- The owner has control and direction over the agent regarding any actions taken by the conventional agent on the behalf of the owner.

Statutory Agency

Statutory agency differs from conventional agency in that:

- A statutory agent does not have the authority to bind the owner personally in other contractual agreements.
- A statutory agent can only bind the owner's property and/ or improvement on the property.
- The actions of a statutory agent are not subject to the control and direction of the owner.

In most states, a statutory agent for the owner of a construction project is called a *construction agent*. The construction agent can be a contractor, architect, builder, lessee, vendee, or any other person having charge of any improvement to real property by written authority of the owner.

If you are given a contract to sign and you do not understand it, either have it reviewed by someone or do not sign it. Never sign what you don't fully understand.

If your pricing is not accurate you may have difficulty collecting any of your shortage from the owner, unless you show that you sought help from the owner and it was denied. From the moment you discover the mistake, begin a paper trail and notify the owner. Document your efforts to get the owner to help correct the mistake.

A construction (statutory) agent has to have a contract with the owner or the owner's conventional agent. This contractual relationship with the owner (or the owner's conventional agent) is what gives the construction agent the authority to make related subcontracts.

These subcontracts have the effect of binding the owner's property, and/or improvement to the property, but not the owner personally.

In other words, subcontractors and others providing performance on the project have the right to a lien on the property and/or improvement. However, they do not have the right to sue the owner personally.

It does not matter that the owner benefits from the work or materials provided. Benefit in itself is not enough to bind the owner or the owner's property.

> ### *Note*
> The following concept is worth repeating: A general contractor, acting as the statutory agent of the owner, does not have the authority to bind the owner personally.
>
> Any subcontract can only result in a lien upon the property and/or improvement. A lien cannot be against an owner personally but only against the owner's property.

Direct Lien System

Some states have adopted a direct lien system. Under the direct lien system, subcontractors and suppliers have lien rights independent of the original contractor.

Making mistakes isn't silly, disregarding them is.

This means that a lien could secure or assure payment of the amount owed a claimant regardless of whether:

- The owner has paid the original contractor
- The original contractor has waived any rights
- The original contractor has breached the contract with the owner

In states without a direct lien system, all claimants have to go through the primary contractor or the person originally contracting with the owner.

Lien Attachment

Attachment is a legal term to describe the act of legally securing property for the purpose of obtaining compensation for a debt.

When a lien is filed in court, it is attached to the property by being recorded as an encumbrance to the property. The property records will show a lien attachment, just as it might show a mortgage attached to it.

A lien arising out of the construction of an improvement attaches principally to the structure itself. Under some circumstances it may also attach to the underlying land or adjacent land as well, subject to restrictions and limitations.

A lien arising out of the performance for land preparation will attach to the land itself. The contractor who performed the improvement only to the land will not be able to claim a lien on a structure built on the same land later by others.

In many states, a lien attaches to the property and/or improvement from the time construction first began. Once the claimant's lien is perfected (or recorded), it will backdate to the beginning of construction (for issues of priority, see "priority," this section), even if construction began before the claimant's performance was furnished.

> **Note**
> The attachment date is an important consideration when determining priority over other interests.

> *The best way to settle a disagreement is on the basis of what's right, not who's right.*

Perfecting a Lien

A claim of lien is perfected when it is filed with the recording officer of the county, or other jurisdiction, in which the improvement or property is located. The statute defines the period within which a claim for lien has to be filed. The period of time is based on the type of performance done.

> **Tip**
> A claim of lien is filed to recover the amount of lienable performance. This is the amount a contractor claims was done under the contract and not paid for. (See *Lienable Performance* in the "Quick Reference Tool".)

A lien has to be perfected within a period of time usually not later than 75 days after performance ceases to be furnished, or 75 days after the completion of construction, whichever is earlier. To file a claim of lien, a person has to have done one of the following:

■ Furnished labor, materials, transportation of materials, or rental equipment used in the construction of an improvement

- Prepared the lot or furnished rental equipment for preparation of land or improvement of an adjoining street

Note

During the balance of this course, we will make reference to time requirements for filing papers and acting to protect your lien rights. States differ in some ways, but generally will use time durations similar to those noted. Check your local requirements if you are filing a lien.

The best way to get rid of your duties is to discharge them.

A lien usually has to be perfected no later than 75 days after completion of construction by every other person claiming a lien. These persons could include:

- Trustee of an employee benefit plan
- Architect
- Landscape architect
- Land surveyor
- Registered engineer

Note

For a definition of *completion of construction,* see Chapter 3: "Statutory Notice Forms and Requirements."

Assignment of Lien

The person who is entitled to a lien may not assign or transfer legal rights to the lien before it is perfected. Until the lien is perfected by public recording, it is considered a personal privilege.

A person receiving an unperfected lien receives an unsecured debt that cannot be perfected in his or her own name because he or she was not the provider of the labor or materials.

Priority

In general, construction lien claimants have equal priority. A construction lien on an improvement generally has priority over all recorded mortgages or trust deeds given for construction financing, provided that the necessary notices have been given to the mortgagee (lender).

If proper notice is not given by those claiming construction liens, the mortgagee may have priority over those claims. The recovery amount for those claiming liens could be reduced by the mortgagee's claim amount.

A construction lien for repair or alteration, however, only has priority over mortgages or deeds of trust given to secure a loan made to finance the alteration or repair of an improvement.

Note

If the proceeds from a foreclosure sale are not enough to pay all the lien claimants, the proceeds generally will be shared pro rata (proportionately distributed) among all valid lien claimants.

Notification Requirements

Under all state lien law statutes, claimants are required to notify owners and interest holders about the:

- Securing of a right to lien
- Perfection of a lien claim
- Foreclosure of lien claims

Proper notification is essential to a fair and efficient lien system. Construction liens are dependent on this notification for their validity.

Note

Careful compliance with the procedures required for the creation and perfection of a lien is important. However, the construction lien statutes are intended to be corrective in nature. Therefore, the courts have held that protection provided for under these statutes will not be undermined if the following conditions are met:

- The claimant provided lienable performance.
- The claimant's deviation from statutory procedure was a good faith and excusable error.
- The deviation from statutory procedure was not contrary to statutory purpose or did not prejudice another's right.

Many contractors get exactly what is coming to them on their projects, but are disappointed to see what it turns out to be.

The statutory notices and requirements are reviewed in great detail in Chapter 3: "Statutory Notice Forms and Requirements."

Extent of Lien

The extent of the lien, or the amount of real property that falls within the lien, is closely related to the distinction between a lien for performance on the improvement and a lien for performance for the land development or preparation.

Land Preparation

Education is what you get from reading the small print in a contract. Experience is what you get from not reading it.

Under most state laws a lien to secure payment for the land or street development attaches to the entire lot. How much land is subject to the lien is dependent upon how much and what portion of the land is required for the convenient use and occupation of the improvement.

For example, the lien on wells extends to the entire property because the wells are intended to benefit the property as a whole. Another example is a lien on farm buildings. The lien extends to the entire lot where the land was used as a farm and to the buildings that were necessary for that use.

Improvement

In contrast to the lien to secure payment for performance for land development or preparation, the lien for improvement attaches to the improvement itself rather than to the property as a whole.
For example, if an owner of a mobile home located on rented land orders (without the land owner's permission) work on the structure, the lien attaches to the mobile home only, not the land.

The land on which the improvement is constructed will only be subject to a lien if the owner of the land caused [requested] the improvement to be constructed.

The landowner who has knowledge of construction on the property will be regarded as having ordered the construction unless a notice of nonresponsibility is posted within three days of obtaining that knowledge. Chapter 3: "Statutory Notice Forms and Requirements" describes this in greater detail.

Well, you did it! You have just completed Chapter 1 which was primarily about the conditions for, and categories of, lienable performance.

Summary

This chapter began with a discussion of the development of lien law statutes and the legal terms used in them and throughout this course. It identified the kinds of construction lien, explained lienable performance, listed the categories of lienable performance, and outlined each. Lastly, it explained the significant principles of construction lien law.

Think of doubt as an invitation to think.

As you go through the following chapters, keep in mind this simple definition of a lien: a lien is a legal right to have property sold or its value applied to the payment of a claim.

A dispute that often results in a lien will deal with an omission. The owner says you did not do all you were supposed to do, and refuses to pay that which is due. Contract documents have to be clear in all aspects of the project, and also have to be clear to the owner. Keep your dispute focused on these documents.

Chapter 2

Contractual Issues

This chapter deals with various aspects of construction contracts that affect a contractor's lien rights. As mentioned in Chapter 1, the right to lien is a statutory right, not a contractual right. However, the lien law statutes assume a contractual relationship exists. Only those persons who provide lienable performance at the request of the owner or owner's agent can enforce their right to lien.

This chapter discusses various aspects of construction contracts that affect a contractor's lien rights, such as:

- Proper and substantial contract performance
- Contract terms that limit, modify, or waive lien rights
- The determination of the amount of the lien
- The effect of claimant's breach of contractual obligations on the right to lien
- Alternatives for contract recovery

Contracts can be verbal or written. Which one do you think makes it possible to prove what you agreed to?

A Contractor's Rights and Obligations

As a construction contractor and wise business person, you will want to protect your:

- Right to lien
- Right to contract enforcement
- Right to claim the full amount owed to you

To protect these rights, you need to attend to three matters before providing labor or services for the improvement of real property. You need to:

- Fulfill all statutory requirements of licensing or registration as a contractor, acquiring necessary bonding and insurance, and completing any prerequisite education.
- Establish that your specific performance is requested by the owner or the owner's agent.

■ Define the work you will perform and the materials you will supply in a valid and enforceable contract.

Proper and Substantial Contract Performance

Proper and substantial performance in the manner specified in the contract is a prerequisite to the claimant's right to lien. A part, or all, of the promises in the contract have to be performed according to the terms and specifications.

To *execute* (or carry through legally) a valid lien, the claimant has to prove that lienable performance was provided in a proper and workmanlike manner. An original contractor also has to show that the performance complied with the contract negotiated between him or her and the owner.

The contract itself may contain prerequisites in addition to performance obligations. For example, the contract may specify that orders for extra work or materials be in writing. In that case, the lien will only cover the additional performance that was ordered in writing. (See *Change Orders* in the "Quick Reference Tool.")

Courts are extremely reluctant to "rewrite" a contract so that either party can revoke the deal that it voluntarily made.

Construction contracts usually call for general conditions, such as installation of a manufactured product. Specifications, details and other requirements of installation have to be communicated and made a part of contract documents in order to be effective in a lien. If a product requires special handling in installation, that information has to get to the installer in a timely way. You can definitely act to avoid this kind of dispute.

Contract Terms That Affect Lien Rights

A person may waive or modify his or her right to claim a lien on lienable performance. This waiver or modification is valid and enforceable, provided that consent is given *voluntarily*. A claimant may waive their lien right expressly or by implication. Close scrutiny of the words or actions of a party is applied before being interpreted as a waiver of lien rights by the courts.

Implied Waiver

An implied lien waiver is one in which the claimant agrees to terms that are clearly inconsistent with the right to lien. For example, a contractor who agrees to take an owner's mortgage to secure the amount due for a construction project waives the right to lien, even if the mortgage is never executed (used). This is because the law regards a mortgage to be inconsistent with the right to lien.

By obtaining a mortgage on the property in question, a contractor waives the right to claim a lien. The right to claim a lien is contingent on no other claim being filed to recover lienable performance.

Terms or agreements that are not waivers of the right to lien include an agreement to arbitrate and an agreement to extend credit, defer payment, or accept a promissory note.

Warning
An agreement to defer payment beyond the period in which a lien has to be foreclosed may be treated as a waiver.

Waiver Limitations

No one ever got hurt on the corners of a square deal.

A party can only be bound by their own lien waiver. A contract clause in which an original contractor agrees not to permit any liens to attach to the property refers to the original contractor's lien rights only.

The lien rights of subcontractors, suppliers, or others providing labor and/or materials are not affected. They cannot be bound by the lien waiver agreed to by the owner and the original contractor who has requested performance from them.

Commercial Construction

An agreement for the construction of a commercial improvement with a provision requiring the original contractor to hold an owner harmless, or to indemnify an owner for a lien created and perfected under the law, is usually enforceable providing one of the following conditions is met:

- A copy of the notice of right to a lien is delivered to the original contractor in person or by certified or registered mail not later than ten days after it is received by the owner.

■ The original contractor has agreed that the owner is not required to deliver a copy of the notice.

■ The claimant who delivered the notice to the owner has a contractual agreement with the original contractor.

Note

Commercial construction lien laws are normally different from residential lien laws. Be sure you know which parts of the state statute apply to residential construction.

Determining the Lien Amount

Before the amount of a lien can be determined, it has to be established that the performance is lienable. (See Chapter 1, "Categories of Lienable Performance.") Once this has been established, the next step is to determine the value of the lienable performance.

Recoverability of Costs

The price stipulated in a contract may be a fixed price or it may be made up of separately priced components. In either case, it most likely is calculated based on the contractor's costs and overhead plus an anticipated profit.

Although all of these costs are recoverable in a contract suit, some of the performance supplied may not be recoverable under the lien law statute.

When the contract does not break the price down into different types of performance, the question becomes whether or not the contractor is obliged to break down the contract price.

Experienced contractors know that it is better to lose a project at the correct price than to get that project at the wrong price.

Note

In many states, the general rule that the contract price is the lien amount does not apply to a renter of equipment.

Under those statutes, the lien for equipment rental is confined to the reasonable rental value of equipment, even if the owner agreed to a higher rental.

Amount of Debt Versus Amount of Lien

In general, the value of one's performance on a construction project will equal the contract amount for the work performed.

Placing a value on lienable performance is governed by state lien law statutes. Recovery of debt for performance is a matter of contract law.

Duty is a task we look forward to with distaste, perform with reluctance, and brag about afterwards.

Under a construction contract, there could be performance by a contractor that was not done on real property. This performance could create a debt that is not lienable because the activity is not a technical legal performance under lien law statutes. A moveable shed built by the contractor under contract, for example, is not real property.

A debt situation could also be created if the owner of the property had the contractor make improvements to the property, but did not have a contract with the claimant.

Sometimes there is a significant difference between the amount of the lien and the amount of debt as contained in the contract price. The contract price may cover such nonlienable items as:

- Credit charges
- Materials not incorporated into or consumed in the construction
- Equipment rental at a higher rate than its reasonable value
- Consequential and other damages

In that case, the lien will secure only part of the debt. A contract claim may be filed to recover debt not secured by the lien. (See "Contract Suit," this chapter.)

Contract with Owner

When lienable performance is provided for in a contract between the owner and the claimant, the contract price is the amount of the lien, excluding exceptions cited above.

When lienable performance is provided for in a contract between the owner and the contractor, the contractor with a lien bears the burden of proving the agreed contract price, for both lien purposes and for recovery in a contract suit.

Tip
Because the burden of proof is on the contractor who is bringing action against an owner, the Academy recommends that all construction contracts be detailed and in writing.

The problem with most verbal contracts: "What you heard is not what I meant."

No Contract with Owner

In most states, the claimant who does not have a contract with the owner acquires a lien only for the reasonable value of labor, services, or material provided.

Lien amounts are not governed by the price quoted in subcontracts. This is because the contractor, acting as statutory agent for the owner, has the power to negotiate subcontracts that can create a lien on the owner's property but cannot bind the owner personally for the subcontract amount.

Practically speaking, the distinction is often of little significance because the subcontract rate is typically based on the market value of the performance. However, this rule protects the owner where there is a discrepancy between subcontract price and market value.

Warning
According to most state case law, at the time of filing a lien claim, the contractor has to separate lienable from nonlienable performance. Failure to do so would result in forfeiture of the lien.

Breach of Contract

A contractual party is said to be in breach of contract when that party fails to fulfill the obligations assigned by the terms and conditions of the contractual agreement.

This means that a party to the contract has to be shown to have deviated from what they promised to do under the contract, or not performed a promised activity under the contract.

A breach of contract by any contractual party, has to be determined to be material (substantial) or immaterial (insubstantial) before the effect on the lien can be known.

Contractor's Material Breach

A contractor can materially breach their contract by:

- Seriously deviating from contract specifications
- Abandoning work without justification
- Otherwise materially breaching the contract.

In all cases the contractor loses their lien rights entirely

"Time is money." Most contracts call for a "time is of the essence" clause. This means delays in project completion may cause the owner a loss. Money loss for construction delays is a common cause of disputes. Use this clause to bring up the subject during negotiations. This will let you know how critical the owner thinks a delay is, and what might happen in resolving a dispute.

Owner's Duty to Object to the Breach

In certain circumstances, the owner has a duty to object to the breach at the time of the improper performance. Failure to object may later prevent (estop) the owner from claiming improper performance.

For example, an owner who supervised the construction project and had some expertise in construction has a duty to object to improper performance at the time it is rendered. This also applies to the owner who, with the assistance of an architect or other expert, could have perceived and objected to the improper work at the time it was done but did not.

It's surprising how often people will agree with you if you just keep your mouth shut.

Contractor's Immaterial Breach

An immaterial or insubstantial breach of contract by the contractor who has substantially performed in good faith will not affect the lien. The contractor will be entitled to a lien for the completed performance amount, adjusted to make allowance for the defects and omissions. Examples of immaterial breach are:

- Not finishing the project by the time specified in the contract
- Using a different, but similar brand of building material

Effect of Contractor's Breach on Other Claimants

Subcontractors or suppliers who supply performance per the general (original) contractor's request can acquire a lien that is independent of the general contractor.

The subcontractor's or supplier's lien is not affected by the general contractor's failure to perform an obligation arising out of a contract to which they were not a party. This is true for breach in general.

Warning

If the general contractor orders performance beyond his or her authority as statutory agent, the general contractor's order may not bind the owner.

While there are many variations, only four main areas of disputes usually occur:

- Costs
- Time
- Errors
- Omissions

Owner's Material Breach

If the contractor fails to complete the work because of the owner's material breach of contract (for example, failure to pay the contractor for completed work) then the contractor will be entitled to a lien for the work done before abandonment. (See "Notice of Abandonment" in Chapter 3, "Statutory Notice Forms and Requirements.")

The lien will secure the full contract price of the project less the value of the work remaining.

Damages Excluded from Lien Amount

The lien covers only the cost of labor, services, or material actually used in constructing an improvement or preparing the land. Additional costs incurred because of the owner's breach of contract usually cannot be recovered by claimants under the lien law.

For example, when the owner's breach results in the delay of other customer's projects, these special damages cannot be recovered under the lien law process.

Warning

Remember, not all breaches will be judged as material. Therefore, not all breaches free the offended party from his or her obligation to perform.

A contractor who abandons a project because of the mistaken belief that the owner is in material breach could, instead, become the breaching party.

Subcontractor's Breach

A subcontractor's or supplier's breach of contract with the general

Many contractors are coming to realize that education is to business what fertilization is to farming.

contractor will not affect a lien filed by them to secure payment for performance rendered by the subcontractor or supplier.

The subcontractor or supplier could have completed lienable performance prior to a breach with the general contractor.

The general contractor may claim damages to compensate for losses resulting from a subcontractor's or supplier's breach. Therefore, a subcontractor's or supplier's subsequent performance may affect the amount they collect under a claim of lien.

The lien amount is based on reasonable value. Performance that is reduced in value because of defects will result in a reduced lien. A defect that is so serious as to render the performance valueless will result in no lien at all. The adequacy of performance provided will be determined by the court, if necessary.

A contractor spent $2,000 replacing an entire fence for an unhappy customer who was still not satisfied. When the customer was finally asked how they wanted the situation handled, they offered a $100 solution.

Alternatives for Contract Recovery

In many cases, a resolution to the amount in question may be more quickly negotiated through a process under contract law. The parties may be disagreeing on a contract issue. This would have to be sorted out prior to the determination of lienable performance.

Contract Suit

Because a contract with either the owner or the owner's statutory agent underlies all lien claims, a contractual party has the option of suing for contract enforcement with, or instead of, lien foreclosure.

A *contract suit* is a court action against the other party of a contract. In a contract suit, parties to the contract are held personally liable to the contractual agreement.

A *lien foreclosure* is a court action to obtain compensation from the property or improvement owned by another party.

Using both options is not a right to recover double payment. Recovery under one action extinguishes the right of recovery under the other action to the extent that it has already been satisfied.

> *Note*
> When suing for contract enforcement is the issue, the original contractor's contractual recovery is against the owner. The subcontractor's or supplier's contractual recovery is against the original contractor.

The action chosen is usually determined by the circumstances of the case. For example, the contract suit may be futile because the liable party may be bankrupt or otherwise judgement proof; or the suit of foreclosure may not be an option because the claimant did not comply with the statutory notification or perfection requirements.

If the claimant loses a right to lien merely because of failure to comply with the lien statute, it will have no affect on the contract claim.

> *Warning*
> If the claimant loses the right to lien because of failure to comply with the state licensing or registration laws, then both the contract claim and the lien claim may be lost.

Quantum Meruit

The general rule for contract recovery is that recovery for performance as specified in the contract is based on the contract price.

A contractor who is in material breach and has lost the right to lien and/or sue for recovery of damages still has possibility of recovery.

In contract law, the concept of quantum meruit is sometimes applied in situations where one party to a contract would "unjustly" prosper at the expense of another.

Quantum meruit translates to, "as much as they deserve." The intent of this concept is to justly and reasonably compensate a party for performance rendered in the absence of the right to lien and/or sue.

Never sign a contract that requires you to do a project quickly, or to get started on one quickly. You will "quickly" have problems.

Warning
The contractor would have the responsibility of proving with reasonable certainty that the work performed was in the best interest of the owner and that the cost of the additional work is reasonable.

A lawyer is always willing to spend your last dollar to prove you're right.

Quasi Contract

The subcontractor, or supplier without a contract with the owner, cannot sue the owner for debt recovery. As mentioned before, the contractor acting as statutory agent of the owner has no power to bind the owner personally.

The subcontractor or supplier loses the right to lien when the performance has been classified as nonlienable or he or she is in noncompliance with statutory notices and perfection requirements.

If this happens and recovery of the debt from the contractor is not possible, the courts will decide whether the claimant has any cause against the owner in quasi contract law.

The *quasi contract* is sometimes referred to as a "contract implied in law." A quasi contract is a court remedy to prevent *unjust enrichment*.

A court may decide to compensate the claimant for the value of a benefit bestowed on the owner to the extent that the owner has been unjustly enriched at the claimant's expense. There are two barriers to a ruling in favor of the subcontractor or materialman in this situation.

Avoid any deal that involves a tax shelter which you benefit from. Later, maybe years later, it could go bad and cost you big money when you have no legal recourse.

- When the owner has already paid the contractor (who did not pay the claimant) and would be paying for the performance twice
- When the claimant could have been protected by complying with the lien statutes and did not comply

Summary

The right to lien is a statutory right, not a contractual right. The lien statutes assume a contractual relationship exists. Only those persons who provide lienable performance at the request of the owner or owner's agent can enforce their right to lien.

Chapter 3

Statutory Notice Forms and Requirements

This chapter covers the statutory notice forms and requirements including delivery and response procedures and time lines, consequences of noncompliance, and mandatory language. It concludes with step-by-step summary charts of the claimant's and the owner's procedures.

No one is very smart who doesn't understand the obvious.

States differ as to notice times, forms and some other details of completing a lien process. The following requirements are representative of a normal process and may include items that are not required in your state.

Notification

All states have extensive statutory notice requirements which are meant to ensure that contractors, and others eligible to claim a lien, adequately inform owners and mortgagees of residential property about the:

- Creation of right to lien
- Perfection of lien claim
- Foreclosure of lien claim

As noted in Chapter 1, notification is essential to a fair and efficient lien system. Construction liens are dependent on proper notification for their validity.

Under the lien statutes, notification is generally required at the following stages of the project:

- At the time the contract is entered into
- During the course of project performance

■ In connection with perfection and foreclosure of the lien

Notices

Different notices are required depending on the nature of the lien and the claimant's contractual relationship with the owner. The forms essential to a lien claim include:

■ Information Notice to Owner About Construction Liens
■ Notice of Right to a Lien
■ Notice to Mortgagee of Delivery of Materials or Supplies
■ Notice of Nonresponsibility
■ Claim of Lien
■ Notice of Claim Filing
■ Notice of Completion
■ Notices of Abandonment and Nonabandonment
■ Notice of Intent to Foreclose Lien

An error doesn't become a mistake until you refuse to correct it.

Construction Lien Book

Under most state lien law statutes, the "Claim of Lien," "Notice of Completion," and "Notice of Abandonment" have to be recorded by the recording officer in the county in which the property is located. These notices are recorded in a construction lien book, a central file for all the lien information you may need.

Noncompliance

All notices required by statute are mandatory, however the consequences of failing to provide proper notice varies. Noncompliance will result in one or more of the following:

■ Forfeiture of the lien
■ Loss of priority
■ Denial of cost and fees

> ### *Note*
> Not all notices need to be sent out by every claimant. Each state has different requirements. Check your state law regarding which notices have to be sent for you to be in compliance.

Information Notice to Owner About Construction Liens

Under most state statutes there is a form that has been adopted similar to the, "Information Notice to Owner About Construction Liens" (Figure 1). This form:

- Warns owners about the lien law
- Describes state lien law in clear, nontechnical language
- Outlines the rights and responsibilities of an owner and a contractor
- Explains the ways in which an owner may avoid multiple payments
- Informs the owner of the right to file a claim against the contractor licensing or registration agency.

Delivery of the "Information Notice to Owner About Construction Liens" is the first step in a correct lien claim filing process, if required.

Tip

Delivery of this form to an owner might have to be proven later. An owner may forget about, or refuse to confirm delivery, of the form.

Staple a copy of the form to your contract when you present it for signing to the owner. Have two sets of contract documents, one for you and one for the owner. Give one set of the signed documents to the owner to keep and keep the other signed set for your files.

If you make a mountain out of a molehill, don't expect anyone to climb up to take in the view.

Delivery

The original construction contractor is usually required under most state laws to give the "Information Notice to Owner" to the owners of residential property in two situations:

- Situation One — Contract price greater than a certain minimum:

    ◆ Written contract. Notice has to be given to the owner when the contract is signed.

- ◆ Oral contract. Notice has to be given to the owner within five days of concluding the contract.
- ◆ Original contract less than the minimum amount. Notice has to be given within five days after the contractor knows or reasonably should know that the price will exceed the minimum amount.

■ Situation Two—First purchaser of residential property

The first purchaser of a residential property is a person who buys a residence within the 75 day period immediately following the completion of construction.

Note
This notice is to inform the purchaser that liens may arise on the property which have not yet been filed. The 75-day period coincides with the 75 days allowed for lien filing after the completion of construction or performance.

Getting the Form

When this type of form is required, they are often available from the licensing or registration agency, sometimes for free. When you are officially a contractor you will receive notice as to how and when you must notify an owner about construction liens. While all states are different on this issue, most require some sort of notice similar to that shown in Figure 1: "Information Notice to Owner About Construction Liens."

Excuses fool no one but the person who makes them.

Notice of Right to a Lien

Most states require that all people hired by a contractor to provide materials, equipment, labor, or services have to give a "Notice of Right to a Lien" to inform an owner about what lienable performance they have provided.

The "Notice of Right to a Lien" informs the owner(s) that lienable work performance in connection with his or her property is being provided. This performance has to be an improvement to a structure on real property or to land preparation.

This notice has to be provided by those who have *not* contracted with the owner directly (subcontractors, suppliers, and others) and whose performance includes:

- Labor
- Land preparation
- Materials
- Rental equipment
- Planning
- Supervision

In a commercial improvement if you have no contract with the owner and have provided labor and materials or materials only, you need to send a "Notice of Right to a Lien" to the owner(s) and mortgagee(s) of the property.

There is an exception to sending a notice in this case; the trustee of an employee benefit plan who acquires a lien for contributions.

Tip
It may be beneficial to send a "Notice of Right to a Lien" to all owners and mortgagees in a residential or commercial improvement even when it is not mandatory.

If your state requires you to file a "Notice of Right to a Lien" during the progress of an improvement, you have to do just that; not before work starts or when completed. As with all requirements of this type, be prepared to prove this with a written record of giving the notice. You can use certified mail.

Noncompliance

Failure to send the "Notice of Right to a Lien" in a timely manner to all owners could affect your claim or lien. You may only be able to claim or lien on the interest owned by the party you have properly notified. A contractor who does not provide the above notice, as required by statute, normally forfeits the right to lien.

One thing about the school of experience; you will repeat the lesson if you flunk the first time.

Figure 1: Sample of Information Notice to Owner About Construction Liens.

INFORMATION NOTICE
TO OWNER
ABOUT CONSTRUCTION LIENS

This is not a lien. It is provided to you by your contractor to advise you about construction lien laws. An Information Notice is not a reflection upon the integrity or credit standing of your contractor. This Information Notice explains the construction lien law and how you can protect your property. As a homeowner, you should read this Information Notice carefully. This Information Notice is required to be given if you contract for residential construction or remodeling or if you are buying a new home, at any time the contract price exceeds $1,000.

If your contractor does not pay subcontractors, laborers, or rental equipment or material suppliers or does not make other legally required payments, those who are owed money can look to your property for payment. **You have the final responsibility for seeing that all bills are paid even if you have paid your contractor in full.**

Under state law, your contractor and others who provide labor, materials, equipment or services to your project *may* be able to claim payment from your property if they have not been paid. *That claim is a construction lien.*

Persons who supply materials, labor, equipment or services ordered by your contractor are permitted by law to record a lien against your property only if they have sent you a timely Notice of Right to a Lien (which is different from this Information Notice) before or during construction. If you enter into a contract to buy a newly-built, a partly-built or a newly-remodeled home, a lien may be claimed even though you have not received a Notice of Right to a Lien.

Common Questions and Answers about Construction Liens

Can someone record a construction lien even if I pay my contractor. Yes. Anyone who has not been paid for labor, material, equipment, or services on your project has provided you with a valid Notice of Right to Lien has the right to record a construction lien.

What is a Notice of Right to a Lien? Persons with whom you do not have a contract are required to send you a Notice of Right to a Lien if they intend to protect their construction lien rights against your project. It is sent to you for your protection. It is not a construction lien.

(Important information on other side)

What should I do when I receive a Notice of Right to a Lien? Don't ignore it. Find out what arrangements are being made to pay the sender of the Notice of Right to a Lien.

When do construction liens need to be recorded? Construction liens generally need to be recorded within 75 days from the date the project was substantially completed or 75 days from the date that the lien claimant ceased to provide labor, material equipment or services, whichever is earlier. To enforce a lien, the lienholder must file a lawsuit in a proper court within 120 days of the date the lien was recorded.

How to Protect Yourself

- When you pay your contractor for materials, labor, equipment or services, you should consider making your checks payable *jointly* to the contractor and whomever sent you a Notice of Right to a Lien.
- You can ask for a statement of the reasonable value of the materials, labor, equipment or services provided to your project from everyone who sends you a Notice of Right to a Lien. If the information is not provided in a timely manner, the sender of the Notice of Right to a Lien may still be able to record a construction lien, but is not entitled to attorney fees.
- Consider using the services of an escrow agent to protect your interests. Consult your attorney to find out whether your escrow agent will protect you against liens when disbursing payments.
- Contact a title company about obtaining a title policy that will protect you from construction lien claims.
- Ask your contractor, lending institution and architect what precautions, if any, they will take to protect your project from construction liens.
- Get evidence that your contractor and those who have sent you a Notice of Right to a Lien have been paid or have waived all their construction lien rights.
- Have a written contract with your contractor. A written contract may be required for your project because it goes over the minimum amount.
- Review a document called Summary: Construction Contractors Law, which your contractor may have to provide to you before work is begun on your residential project.
- Call your contractor licensing or registration agency for information on your contractor's license or registration status. Other information may be available on dispute resolution and how to file claims.
- Consult an attorney. If you do not have an attorney, consider contacting your State Bar referral service.

Signing this Information Notice indicates only that you have received it. Your signature does not, in any way, give your contractor or those who provide material, labor, equipment or services any additional rights to place a lien on your property.

Job Site Address: _____

This Notice was Furnished by: Received by:

_____   _____
(Contractor)   *(Owner(s))*

_____   _____
(License or Registration #)   (Date)   *(Date)*

Noncompliance

Failure to deliver the "Information Notice to Owner," as specified by statute, can be a statutory violation for which the licensing or registration agency may revoke the contractor's license registration or impose civil penalties.

Confusion with Information Notice

Contractors have sometimes confused the "Notice of Right to a Lien" with the "Information Notice to Owners."

In most states only the delivery of "Information Notice to Owners" is mandatory for the original (general) contractor when contracting a residential project.

There are a lot of "hot" arguments over "cold" cash.

The delivery of a "Notice of Right to a Lien" is not always mandatory. There are no consequences, such as a civil penalty and/or revocation of license or registration certificate. The only consequence for failure to provide the "Notice of Right to a Lien" is forfeiture of the right to a lien.

Again, the "Notice of Right to a Lien" is required for lien purposes and not always mandatory as the "Information Notice to Owners" is.

Tip

Protect your right to lien by issuing this notice as soon as possible to the appropriate parties of your construction projects.

Delivery

The "Notice of Right to a Lien" has to be in writing and has to be delivered in person or by registered or certified mail.

Effective Date

The statute does not usually specify that the notice be given within a certain time frame. However, it excludes from a lien any performance provided before the effective date of the notice. The effective date of the notice normally begins eight business days (excluding weekends and holidays) before the date notice is given. Therefore, notice given late will diminish the lien, not invalidate it.

> ### Warning
> If the claimant furnishes material one day before the project is complete, notice has to be given before completion of construction if it were to occur on the next day. In this case, there are not seven additional days in which to give notice.
>
> Under most state lien law statutes, the "Notice of Right to a Lien" has to be given while the contractor is still engaged in the process of construction.

Noncompliance

If a subcontractor or supplier does not deliver this notice to an owner, they usually waive the ability to claim a lien in the future. Any payment due would likely have to be litigated in court based on other agreements they might have with the owner.

Language

The language that has to be contained in the "Notice of Right to a Lien" is prescribed under your state lien law statutes. The notice has to fully describe the transaction by including the:

- Labor, services, equipment, and materials supplied
- Location of the property
- Name, address, and telephone number of the claimant
- Name of the person who ordered the work and the materials

An expert knows the answers all right, if you ask the right questions.

The notice also has to disclose legal implications, such as:

- Nature and extent of the lien
- Danger that the lien may arise in spite of payment to the general contractor
- Steps the owners might take to protect interests

The "Notice of Right to a Lien" (Figure 2) conforms to most statutory requirements. You may use this form, purchase one from a stationery supply store, or devise your own form that complies with statutory requirements.

Figure 2: Sample of Notice of Right to a Lien

NOTICE OF RIGHT TO A LIEN

**Warning: Read this notice.
Protect yourself from paying any contractor or supplier
twice for the same service.**

To: _____   Date of mailing: _____
       (Owner)   *(by certified mail)*

_____

_____
       (Owner's Address)

This is to inform you that _____ (name of contractor)

has begun to provide _____

_____

(description of materials, equipment, labor, or services) ordered by_____

for improvements to property you own. The property is located at _____

A lien may be claimed for all materials, equipment, labor, and services furnished after a date that is eight days, not including Saturdays, Sundays and other holidays, as defined in state law, before this notice was mailed to you.

Even if you or your mortgage lender have made full payment to the contractor who ordered these materials or services, your property may still be subject to a lien unless the supplier providing this notice is paid.

THIS IS NOT A LIEN. It is a notice sent to you for your protection in compliance with the construction lien laws of the State.

This notice has been sent to you by:

Name:_____

Address:_____

Telephone: _____

*If you have any questions about this notice, feel free to call us.
See reverse side for more important information about how to protect yourself.*

IMPORTANT INFORMATION
FOR YOUR PROTECTION

Under this state's laws, those who work on your property or provide labor, equipment, services, or materials and are not paid have a right to enforce their claim for payment against your property. This claim is known as a construction lien.

If your contractor fails to pay subcontractors, material suppliers, rental equipment suppliers, service providers, or laborers or neglects to make other legally required payments, the people who are owed money can look to your property for payment, *even if you have paid your contractor in full.*

The law states that all people hired by a contractor to provide you with materials, equipment, labor, or services must give you a *Notice of Right to a Lien* to let you know what they have provided.

How to Protect Yourself

- Recognize that this *Notice of Right to a Lien* may result in a lien against your property unless all those supplying a *Notice of Right to a Lien* have been paid.
- When you pay your contractor for materials, labor, equipment or services, you should consider making your checks payable jointly to the contractor and whomever sent you a *Notice of Right to a Lien.*
- You can ask for a statement of the reasonable value of labor, equipment or services provided to your property from each party that sends you a *Notice of the Right to a Lien.* If the information is not provided in a timely manner, the sender of the *Notice of Right to a Lien* may still be able to record a construction lien, but is not entitled to attorney fees.
- Consider using the services of an escrow agent to protect your interests. Consult your attorney to find out whether your escrow agent will protect you against liens when disbursing payments.
- Contact a title company about obtaining a title policy that will protect you from construction lien claims.
- Ask your contractor, lending institution and architect what precautions, if any, they will take to protect your project from construction liens.
- Get evidence that your contractor and those who have sent you a Notice of a Right to a Lien have been paid or have waived all their construction lien rights.
- Have a written contract with your contractor. A written contract may be required for a project over a certain minimum.
- Learn more about the lien laws and the meaning of this notice by requesting a brochure from your licensing or registration agency.
- Call your contractor licensing or registration agency for information on your contractor's license or registration status. Other information is available on dispute resolution and how to file claims.
- Consult an attorney. If you do not have an attorney, consider contacting your State Bar referral service.

Preparing the Owner

Both the "Information Notice to Owners" and the "Notice of Right to a Lien" can have an alarming effect on the owner of a residential project. Most owners will not understand the lien law process simply by reading the notice.

The Academy recommends that steps be taken by general contractors and subcontractors to prepare the owner regarding these forms and the information set forth.

Original contractors may want to reassure the customer that distribution of the "Information Notice to Owner" is simply a state-mandated procedure. Remind customers that you are a professional and responsible contractor and that you are willing to provide them with proof that the bills are being paid.

Explain to owners the likelihood of receiving a "Notice of Right to a Lien." Reassure them that these do not constitute an actual lien and that this too is a statutory requirement.

Original contractors may also want to request that subcontractors and suppliers send a brief cover letter along with the "Notice of Right to a Lien," reassuring owners of the contractor's good standing with them.

> In most cases, all an argument proves is that there are two people present.

Owner's Response to Notice Delivery

After receiving a "Notice of Right to a Lien," the owner may demand, in writing:

- A list of materials or equipment
- Description of labor or services supplied
- A statement taken from the contract on the basis of which materials, equipment, services, or labor were provided

The supplier is normally required by law to provide the owner with information requested within 15 business days from the date the request is received. If the supplier does not respond within the period specified, he or she can forfeit attorney's fees and costs that would have been allowed in a foreclosure suit.

> ***Tip***
> If you are a general contractor, you may want to compose this cover letter yourself and request that your subcontractors and suppliers send it with their notice.

Waiver of Construction Lien

In every case where a subcontractor or supplier delivers a "Notice of Right to Lien" to your customer, get a "Waiver of Construction Lien" when the account is paid. (See figure 3, sample of "Waiver of Construction Lien.")

When your bill or account is paid, the subcontractor or supplier has no further right to lien. Insist that you receive a copy of the "Waiver of Construction Lien" that the subcontractor or supplier sent to your customer regarding the "Notice of Right to Lien."

> **Note**
> You may want the subcontractor or supplier to have the "Waiver of Construction Lien" prepared, so you can get it when you pay. Exchange your check for the completed form, then you can send it to your customer with a cover letter.

A sure way to stop a hot argument is to lay a few cold facts on it.

Noncompliance

If the owner fails to request a list and description of materials and labor supplied, the contractor has no obligation to inform the owner of the details in the claim of lien.

Notice to Mortgagee of Delivery of Materials or Supplies

A mortgagee is a person who has an existing valid mortgage of record or trust deed of record that secures a loan on land or an improvement. All mortgagees and other security interest holders are recorded on property records in the county where the property lies.

Anyone who provides materials or supplies for the improvement of real property is required to provide a notice of delivery of materials

Figure 3: Sample Waiver of Construction Lien

Waiver of Construction Lien

Property Owner _____

Address _____

Contractor _____

Address _____

To whom it may concern_____
(Name of firm)

has been employed by_____
(Name of contractor)

 to furnish_____

_____

for the building or property with the address

of_____

_____

City of_____   County of_____

State of_____   Lot no._____

Section_____   Township_____ Range_____

Now that _____

the undersigned, has received the full and complete considerations due, receipt acknowledged, I waive and

release any and all lien, or right to lien on the above described building and property under the statutes of

the state of _____ relating to construction liens, on account of labor or materials, or both,

furnished or to be furnished, by the undersigned to or on account of

_____

 for said building or property.

Witnessed this_____ day

of_____,19_____

Signature_____Witness_____

Title_____

to any mortgagee (including trust deed holders) whose encumbrance on the land or improvement was recorded at the time the materials or supplies were furnished.

Any deal that is too good to be true is. Leave it alone!

Delivery

This notice ordinarily has to be delivered not later than eight business days after the date of delivery of materials or supplies. The notice has to be delivered in person or by registered or certified mail.

Noncompliance

If the notice is not given to the mortgagee who is entitled to it, any priority the lien would have had over any other claim on the property will be lost. For more information refer to the section "Priority" in Chapter 1, "Lien Law Simplified."

Warning

Claimants may be able to give the "Notice of Right to a Lien" to owners at any stage of the performance. State statutes usually do not allow for late delivery of "Notice of Right to a Lien" to mortgagee(s).

Language

A copy of the "Notice of Right to a Lien" will satisfy this requirement. If another form is used, it has to contain the same information contained in the "Notice of Right to a Lien."

Mortgagee's Response to Delivery

Like the owner, the mortgagee may request additional information after receiving the notice. The mortgagee may demand a:

- List of materials and supplies
- Statement of the amount due

The supplier is required to furnish the mortgagee with information requested within 15 days from the date the request was received.

Noncompliance

If the supplier does not provide this information within the period specified, any priority he or she may have had over other claims on the property will be waived.

Notice of Nonresponsibility

A land owner with the knowledge of a construction project that they did**not** order may be required to post a "Notice of Nonresponsibility," (Figure 4). This notice warns suppliers that the land owner will not be responsible for performance ordered by the occupier of the land.

Posting By Land Owner

The land owner may be required to post this notice in a conspicuous place on the land or improvement within three days after becoming aware of the construction project. The statute does not usually require that the notice be dated or signed.

> ### Note
> The notice relates to the erection of an improvement, not land preparation. This notice can only be effectively given by the owner of the land, not the owner of the improvement.

Noncompliance

If the land owner with the knowledge of the construction project does not post a notice of nonresponsibility containing the information required within the period specified, the provider of the lienable performance will acquire the right of lien on the land.

Language

Figure 4 provides a sample of a "Notice of Nonresponsibility" that complies with most statutory requirements.

Claim of Lien

A lien is perfected by filing a "Claim of Lien" (Figure 5) with the recording officer in the county in which the real property is located.

Anyone who claims a lien has to perfect the lien not later than 75 days after labor, rental equipment, or materials are furnished, or 75 days after construction is completed, whichever is earlier. (See

"Notice of Completion," this section.) The form has to include:

- A true statement of demand after deducting the credits and offsets
- The name of the owner or reputed owner, if known
- The name of the person who employed the claimant or to whom performance was furnished or who is owing for the contributions
- A description of the property, including the address if known

Language

The "Claim of Lien" form shown in Figure 5, conforms to many statutory requirements. The form is drafted for a claim of lien by the contractor, subcontractor, or supplier who has provided labor, supplied or transported materials, or rented equipment for use in the construction of an improvement.

Cost estimates, and owner approval, of all proposed changes will keep owners from balking later when billed for the work.

You may use this form, purchase one at a stationery supply store, or devise your own form to comply with statutory requirements.

Duration

The "Claim of Lien" binds the property for a period of 120 days after it is recorded. This time may be extended if there is an agreement for extended payment and this agreement is stated in the "Claim of Lien."

The maximum period of extension is around two years from the time the "Claim of Lien" is recorded.

Note
This form has to be modified to make it applicable to:

- The claimant who provided labor, materials, or equipment for the preparation of land or the improvement of an adjoining street
- Trustee of an employee benefit plan
- An architect, landscape architect, and others claiming a lien for planning or supervision of an improvement or land preparation

Figure 4: Sample of Notice of Nonresponsibility

NOTICE OF NONRESPONSIBILITY

_____

(name)

_____

(address)

the owner of (if not owner of full title, the holder of a described interest in property) (description of property)

_____

_____

gives notice that any improvement constructed upon the above property has not been and is not being constructed at (his/her/its) instance or request. (He/She/It) is not and will not be responsible for any labor, materials, services, or equipment provided or to be provided in connection with any such construction on the property.

This notice is posted on the above property on

_____ .

Dated_____ , 19_____

_____

(signature)

Notice of Claim Filing

After a claimant has filed a lien, he or she has to give notice of the filing to the owner(s) and the mortgagee(s). The reason for notice is to give owners and mortgagees an opportunity to settle the lien before litigation or to take other protective measures, such as withholding funds that would have been paid out to a contractor.

In legal matters, the difference between failure and success is doing a thing almost right and doing it exactly right.

Delivery

The notice has to be in writing and has to be delivered in person or sent by registered or certified mail to owners and mortgagees within 20 days of the filing of the "Claim of Lien." A copy of the "Claim of Lien" has to be attached to the notice.

> ***Note***
> Unlike the "Notice of Right to a Lien," the "Notice of Claim Filing" has to be sent out to all owners, whether or not a contractual relationship exists, as well as all persons with a valid existing mortgage of record or trust deed of record securing a loan on land or an improvement.

Noncompliance

Failure to give notice to owners and mortgagees usually does not affect the validity of the lien. However, noncompliance will often result in the loss of costs and fees that would have been allowed in a foreclosure suit.

Language

Most statutes do not prescribe the contents of the notice, only that notice has to be given. The "Notice of Claim Filing" (Figure 6) provides owners and mortgagees with adequate notice. This information may also be expressed in letter form.

Owner's Response to Delivery

The owner(s) may respond to the filing by establishing a separate bond or cash deposit with the county's recording officer.

This bond or cash deposit can be used by the owner to demand

Figure 5: Sample of appropriate Claim of Lien for claimant providing labor, rented equipment, or materials

CLAIM OF LIEN

Please take notice that _____(claimant)_____, the claimant, claims a construction lien on the following real property situated in _____ County, State of _____:
   (description of property sufficient for identification)

1. The address of property is (if unknown, state so)_____

    _____

2. The owner(s) or reputed owner(s) of the property is (are) <u>(if more than one owner, state names of all owners whose interests are to be bound).</u> [Or, if the ownership of the improvement is different from that of the land:

    The owner(s) or reputed owner(s) of the land is (are)

    The owner(s) or reputed owner(s) of the improvement erected on the land is (are)

3. The Claimant's lien is claimed for labor provided/materials furnished (or transported)/equipment rented by the claimant under a contract with _____who is (are)owner(s) of the land/improvement [or contractor/ agent/construction agent of the owner of the land/ improvement].

    Under that contract, Claimant was employed by /furnishing materials/renting equipment to [This will usually be the person named in the first blank space of Paragraph 3.]

4. The labor was provided/materials furnished (or transported)/equipment rented in connection with the following improvement on the property

5. The Claimant commenced to perform the labor/furnish (or transport) the materials/ rent the equipment on __(date)__ and completed such performance on __(date)__ .

(continued...)

6. The amount of the lien claimed by the Claimant, after the deduction of all just credits and   offsets is $_____, as shown in the following statement of demand:

Contract price (or reasonable value) of the

labor/materials/transport/equipment   _____

(describe and itemize performance)   _____

Subtotal   Plus recording fees   _____

Subtotal   Plus recording fees   _____

 Total

The Claimant therefore claims a lien on the property described above, extending to the improvement and its site, together with so much of the land as may be required for the convenient use and occupation of the improvement, to be determined by the court at the time of foreclosure of this lien.

Dated _____, 19_____   _____(claimant's signature)

State of _____, Country of _____ ss.

I _____, being first duly sworn, depose and say that:

I am the Claimant/_(capacity, if representative)_ of the Claimant named in the above claim of lien. I have knowledge of the facts set forth in the claim of lien. I believe that all statements made in the claim of lien are true and correct.

Subscribed and sworn to before me this _____day of _____,19_____.

_____

Notary Public for_____

My commission expires_____

transfer of the lien encumbrance from the property to the bond holder or cash deposit. For more information about the effect this has upon claimant's liens, consult your state lien law.

An owner would use this process to keep the property free of a recorded encumbrance. This would be most useful if a sale is pending or if a mortgagee would object to an encumbrance on the property.

Experience may not be worth the price, but it's hard to get cheaply.

Warning

Under certain conditions, the claimant could become liable for costs accrued by the owner or mortgagee in making the demand to release the lien by transferring the encumbrance to the bond holder or cash deposit. For this reason, filing a frivolous lien could be costly to the claimant.

Notice of Completion

As mentioned in the "Claim of Lien," persons performing some types of lienable performance have to perfect a lien claim within 75 days of completion of the improvement.

What is Completion?

An improvement is considered complete if any of the following apply:

- The improvement is substantially complete.
- A "Notice of Completion" is posted on the improvement and recorded with the county.
- A "Notice of Abandonment" or "Nonabandonment" is posted on the improvement and recorded with the county.

Language

The contents of the "Notice of Completion" are usually prescribed under state statutes. Figure 7 is an example of a "Notice of Completion" that is in compliance with many state statutes.

Posting By Owner

An improvement is considered abandoned on the 75th day after construction work on the improvement ceases, or when the owner or mortgagee of the improvement, or agent of either, posts and records a "Notice of Abandonment." The notice has to be in writing and signed by the owner or mortgagee.

Affidavit of Posting

An "Affidavit of Posting" needs to accompany the copy of "Notice of Completion" when recorded with the county.

Figure 8, is an example of an "Affidavit of Posting."

Notice of Abandonment

The "Notice of Abandonment" declares that the construction is stopped on a specific project. The property owner, agent, or mortgagee can post this notice to notify interested parties that work has been stopped.

On the 75th day after work on a project has ceased, the project is automatically considered abandoned. At this time, or at the time of posting notice, claims for liens can be filed.

Posting By Owner

Many people believe in law and order as long as they can lay down the law and give the orders.

The "Notice of Abandonment" has to be posted in a conspicuous place on the land or improvement on the same date it was signed. Within five days of the posting, the party posting the notice has to record a copy of the notice along with an "Affidavit of Posting" in the county where the property is located.

> **Note**
> The original contractor cannot post or record a "Notice of Abandonment."

Language

The contents of the "Notice of Abandonment" are usually prescribed under the statutes. Figure 9 is an example of a "Notice of Abandonment" that complies with statutory requirements.

Notice of Nonabandonment

A "Notice of Nonabandonment" is used to inform the public that construction on an improvement has not been stopped.

Posting By Owner

The notice needs to be in writing, signed by the owner or mortgagee, and posted on the same date it was signed in a conspicuous place on the land or improvement. Within five days of posting, a copy of the notice, with an "Affidavit of Posting," has to be recorded in the county in which the property is situated. This needs to happen no later than the 74th day after construction ceases. The "Notice of Nonabandonment" can be renewed at intervals of 150 days by rerecording the notice. The contents of the notice are prescribed in your state lien law. Figure 10, is an example of a "Notice of Nonabandonment" that conforms with most state statutes.

Notice of Intent to Foreclose

After the "Claim of Lien" has been filed and construction has been abandoned, the next principal step in lien enforcement is the foreclosure suit.

The "Notice of Intent to Foreclose" lets the owner know that the claimant intends to foreclose on the lien. The claimant has to give owners an opportunity to avoid foreclosure by paying the lien or providing a bond and give mortgagees the opportunity to take protective measures to protect their security.

Don't use your dog's admiration as proof that you know what you are doing in your business.

Delivery

The claimant has to give any owner and mortgagee(s) with a valid existing mortgage or trust deed on the property notice of intention to foreclose at least ten (10) days prior to the foreclosure action.

Language

Most statutes do not prescribe the language of the notice. The only requirement relating to the content of the notice is that it state that the claimant, or others, intend to begin suit to foreclose the lien. Figure 11 is an example of a "Notice of Intent to Foreclose Lien" that complies with most statutory requirements. This information may also be expressed in letter form.

Owner's Response to Notice of Intent to Foreclose

After receiving the "Notice of Intent to Foreclose Lien," the owner, but not the mortgagee, may demand a list of materials and supplies that reflect the claim amount or a statement of the contractual basis of the obligation that is subject to the suit.

Consistent efforts to communicate and cooperate at the beginning of the project can help greatly in keeping disputes from occurring.

Noncompliance

The claimant needs to furnish the information requested within five days of the demand. Failure to provide the owner with notice or respond to the owner's request for information will not invalidate the lien. However, the claimant will lose any right to costs or attorney's fees that would have been allowed in the foreclosure suit.

Summary

This concludes Chapter 3. This chapter covered the statutory notice forms and requirements including delivery and response procedures and time lines, consequences of noncompliance, and mandatory language. It concludes with step-by-step summary charts of both the claimant's and the owner's procedures.

Figure 6: Sample of Notice of Claim Filing

NOTICE OF CLAIM FILING

To: _____
(owner)

_____
(address)

and

To: _____
(mortgagee)

_____
(address)

You are given notice that on_____,
the original claim of lien, a copy of which is
attached, was filed by_____in
the recording office of_____
County, State of _____.

_____
(claimant)

_____
(address)

[Attach an accurate copy of the claim.]

Figure 7: Sample of Notice of Completion

NOTICE OF COMPLETION

Notice is hereby given that the building structure or other improvement on the following described premises:

(insert legal description of the property, including

street address, if known) has been completed.

All persons claiming a lien upon the same under the Construction Lien Law hereby are notified to file a claim of lien as required by state statute.

Dated_____ ,19_____

_____
General Contractor/Owner/Mortgagee

By:_____

P.O./Address_____

_____

Figure 8: Sample of Affidavit of Posting

AFFIDAVIT OF POSTING

State of _____, County of _____ss.

I,_____, being duly sworn depose and say that: I am the (agent of _____,
the primary contractor for the improvement erected on the property described in the above notice or alternatively, I am the (agent of _____,
the owner/mortgagee of the property described in the above notice).

On _____ , 19_____, I posted the original notice, of which the above (attached) notice is a true copy, on the property described above.

I posted the notice by <u>(state the manner of affixation)</u> it on/at the <u>(state the location, on the structure, or</u> the land of posting).

Subscribed and sworn to before me this _____ day of

_____, 19_____.

_____
Notary Public for _____
My commission expires_____

Figure 9: Sample of Notice of Abandonment

NOTICE OF ABANDONMENT

Notice is hereby given that the building structure or other improvement on the following described premises:

(insert legal description of the property, including street address, if known) has been abandoned.

All persons claiming a lien upon the same under the Construction Lien Law hereby are notified to file a claim of lien as required by state statute.

Dated _____ , 19_____

Owner/Mortgagee _____

By: _____

P.O./Address _____

Figure 10: Sample of Notice of Nonabandonment

NOTICE OF NONABANDONMENT

Notice is hereby given that the improvement in the course of erection on the following described premises has not been abandoned <u>(insert legal description of property, including street address, if   known).</u>

Although work on the construction of the improvement has ceased, it has been delayed for the following reasons <u>(state reasons for the delay in construction.</u> The owner (mortgagee) intends to resume construction.

Dated_____ , 19_____

_____
Owner/Mortgagee

By:_____

P.O./Address_____

Figure 11: Sample of Notice of Intent to Foreclose Lien,

NOTICE OF INTENT TO FORECLOSE LIEN

owner)

To:_____

(address)

_____

and

To:_____
(mortgagee)

(address)

_____

On __(date)__ , __(claimant)__ filed a construction lien on (description

of property). _____

The lien is for the amount of $ _____ for (describe nature of perfor-

mance—for example, labor furnished in the construction of an

improvement on the property) ordered by (name the person ordering the

performance)

You are given notice that unless full payment is received, claimant [or

other person intending to commence suit] intends to commence suit to

foreclose the lien ten (10) days after the date of delivery of this notice.

Dated_____19_____

_____

Claimant

By: _____

Action	Explanation
1. Comply with registration requirements for construction contractors.	Inquire about your state's requirements
2. Prepare claimant's contract.	Contracts protect both your customer and yourself.
3. Provide "Information Notice to Owner About Construction Liens."	Residential property only. Provided to owner by original contractor when contract exceeds certain minimums or to purchaser of new residence if purchased within 75 days of completion. Has to be delivered in person with contract documents, or in some cases mailed or delivered after contract is concluded. Penalty for noncompliance—loss of right to lien; possible revocation of license or registration and civil penalty .
4. Commence construction.	Lien attaches.
5. Commence Claimant's performance.	Begins lienable performance
6. Provide "Notice of Right to a Lien."	Provided to owner by a claimant who does not have a contract with the owner. (Note: except commercial improvements.) May be given at any time during the performance. Covers performance beginning eight business days before the date of notice. Delivery in person or by certified or registered mail.

7.	Waiver of Construction Lien.	When bill or account of supplier or subcontractor is paid in full by the contractor, ask for this waiver. Show owner a copy of the waiver to prove a lien can no longer be filed.
8.	Deliver "Notice to Mortgagee of the Delivery of Materials and Supplies."	Penalty for noncompliance—loss of right to a lien.
		Provided to prior mortgagee by all claimants who provide material or supplies (whether or not labor also is provided).
		Has to be given within eight business days of first delivery of materials or supplies.
		Notice can be a copy of "Notice of Right to a Lien."
		Delivery in person or by certified or registered mail.
		Penalty for noncompliance—loss of priority of claim.
9.	Respond to owner's demands following delivery of notice.	Has to provide within 15 business days a list of materials or description of labor, on demand.
		Has to provide within 15 business days of receipt of demand a list of materials and supplies and statement of amount due.
10.	Respond to mortgagee's demands following delivery of notice.	Penalty for noncompliance—loss of priority.

11. File "Claim of Lien."

Claimants who furnish labor, rental equipment, or material need to file a claim within 75 days of cessation of performance or completion of construction, whichever is earlier.

Other claimants need to file within 75 days of completion of construction.

(Completion or abandonment of construction may be fixed by the owner's posting and recording of notice.

May occur only after filing.

12. Assign lien (optional).

A contractor may assign (transfer interest) in a claim of lien to another party. This would relieve the contractor of collection under the lien. The assignee would collect the lien proceeds as the recorded interest holder.

13. Provide "Notice of Claim Filing."

Provided to owner and mortgagee after lien filing by all claimants.

Has to be mailed within 20 days of filing.

Penalty for noncompliance — costs and fees forfeited.

14. Provide "Notice of Intent to Foreclose."

Provided by all claimants to owner and mortgagee at least 10 days before commencement of foreclosure suit.

Has to be delivered personally or by registered mail.

Penalty for noncompliance—costs and fees forfeited.

15. Respond to owner's demands following delivery of notice.

The claimant needs to furnish the information requested (list of materials, supplies or contractual basis for claim) within five days of the demand.

Penalty for noncompliance—costs and fees forfeited.

16. Commence foreclosure suit.

The suit has to be commenced within 120 days of filing the "Claim of Lien."

If credit terms are recorded in the "Claim of Lien," suit has to be commenced within 120 days from expiration of the credit. Maximum limitation is two years from "Claim of Lien" filing.

Owner

Action	Explanation
1. Post "Notice of Nonresponsibility."	Has to be posted within 3 days of landowner's acquiring knowledge of construction of an improvement not being erected at his instance.
2. Respond to delivery of "Notice of Right to a Lien."	Optional demand for list of materials and description of labor.
	Copy of "Notice of Right to a Lien" to be given to the primary contractor (one who waives right to lien), if appropriate.
3. Post notices of completion, abandonment, or nonabandonment.	May be filed respectively upon completion, abandonment, or upon construction being delayed temporarily.
4. Respond to delivery of "Notice of Claim Filing."	Owner may file a bond or cash deposit and demand release of lien from the property or improvement.
	Once bond or cash deposit has been filed with the county, notice needs to be given to claimant within 20 days.
5. Respond to delivery of "Notice of Intent to Foreclose."	Demand a list of materials or supplies, or contractual basis of claim, (optional).

Chapter 4

Alternatives to Lien Action

Remember, the contract governs what you can do and ask for. If your contract will not support your demands, no court will either.

This chapter includes several alternatives to the lien law process. Ways to prevent a dispute include defining specific performance in a contract and developing useful communication skills. Three alternatives for securing payment for performance include suing the contractor's bond, filing a claim with the licensing or registration agency, and submitting a dispute to an arbitration or mediation organization for resolution.

Dispute Prevention

As a construction contractor seeking longevity and profitability in the construction contracting business, you should consider dispute prevention as an essential business tool.

A dispute between yourself and another party to a contract, that cannot be settled in a friendly manner, will result in business losses that will not be apparent at the time of the dispute.

For example, your business profitability can be affected negatively by:

- Bad publicity from clients
- Lack of repeat business from clients
- Lack of referral business from clients

Two important ways to prevent disputes include using good communication skills and a well formulated contract.

Disputes do not get better with age. Your best bet when a dispute arises is to handle it quickly and get a resolution. Lien law is a big stick for you to use to collect money. However, your relationship with a customer will be destroyed.

Communication Skills

Disputes between parties performing work on a construction project, in all but a few cases, can be prevented by clear communication.

One very effective technique is to repeat what a party just said to be certain that you understood it correctly. Ways to preface your reply to important issues include:

- "Do you mean that ..."
- "Are you saying that ..."
- "If I understand you correctly ..."

Encourage the other party to do the same thing with you. This may seem like a silly waste of time, but not when you consider that most disputes occur because people are not "speaking the same language."

Communicate Important Facts

Anything you, the contractor, can do to address the owner's concerns will go a long way toward preventing disputes. Some important items to communicate to the owner include:

- Your license or registration with the correct agency
- The owners' rights through the claims process
- The performance standards which you adhere to on the job
- A list of references for similar work
- The fact that work by subcontractors will be done according to a written contract
- Your willingness to answer questions pertaining to the project
- The importance of communicating all concerns immediately

Seek out agreement on something minor and then write it down so it will not be forgotten. Build on this agreement.

Clear communication before and during construction is essential to a successful project.

In negotiations there is a big difference between taking a position and pursuing an interest. In taking a position, you state you must get a specific result; this can easily block progress. By pursuing an interest, you can leave yourself open to options in gaining your interest, this allows for many more opportunities to find mutual resolutions of interest.

A Well-Formulated Contract

In dispute resolution and prevention, it is best to keep emotions at bay. Instead, use specific details of your contract and other information that is absolutely clear.

As valuable as good communication skills are, you cannot negate the value of a well-formulated contract. As a construction contractor, a residential construction contractor's agreement is one of your fundamental tools for preventing disputes.

A contract does not have to be a complex document. However, it should be written so that the rights and duties of each party are clearly understood and are enforceable.

General Contractor/Owner

Your residential construction contractor's agreement with the owner should be the result of a negotiation process between yourself and the owner. Good communication skills will facilitate this process. This contract will need to address basic legal considerations as well as issues particular to the project.

General Contractor/Subcontractor

As the general contractor, you should also have a written contractual agreement with all subcontractors on the project. Contractors who perform work for each other without written subcontract agreements may become liable for the negligence of others.

The American Institute of Architects (AIA) has a document A201 which is used as the basis for relationships between all parties to a contract. It focuses on using mediation processes at the earliest stage of a dispute. Most large projects have some kind of dispute during construction. Using this form in your contract documents can set a mediation process for your projects.

Securing Payment for Performance

In addition to claiming a lien and/or suing for contract enforcement, there are other options for securing payment for performance rendered. The options available will vary based upon the type of performance rendered, reason for claim, and amount of claim.

Depending on the circumstances, you may be able to secure payment through one of these three methods:

- Suing the contractor's bond
- Filing a claim with the licensing or registration agency
- Alternative dispute resolution

Suing the Contractor's Bond

The possibility of suing the contractor's surety bond is one option for securing payment for performance provided in a construction project. This method will work for general contractors suing subcontractors, and subcontractors suing general contractors.

> Anyone who has worked on a construction project knows how uncertain it is to predict exact results. Unfortunately, this is something the owner ordinarily does not know. You can educate the owner and keep disputes to a minimum.

Public Protection

Most construction contractors are required to be licensed or registered with an agency that regulates contractors. The purpose of the licensing or registration requirement is to protect the public and other contractors from unreliable, fraudulent, or irresponsible construction contractors. The law is also intended to protect those who supply construction contractors with labor, services, or materials.

Two of the most significant requirements relating to public protection are the bonding and insurance obligations for contractors.

To get licensed or registered, most states require construction contractors to obtain:

- Public liability and property damage insurance to cover liability arising out of work performance
- A surety bond that will pay for any claims arising out of:

  - Improper work
  - Breach of contract
  - Failure to pay persons performing labor or furnishing material or equipment for construction

The Contractor's Bond

If a contractor breaches payment or performance obligations guaranteed by that contractor's bond, the persons to whom the obligation was owed (owner, laborer, supplier, subcontractor or general contractor) can sue that bond.

Note

In some cases, a claim against a general contractor or specialty contractor will automatically bring a court action upon the contractor's bond.

The amount of the bond is dictated by the agency that licenses or registers contractors. Amounts of bonds vary, depending on the type or amount of work done. Typical bond amounts are:

- $2,000 for a limited contractor
- $5,000 for a specialty contractor
- $10,000 for a general contractor

Although the surety bond is not adequate for large claims, it does provide additional protection to subcontractors and suppliers who have a right of recourse against the bond, as well as a lien on the property, and a personal claim against the general contractor.

Note

In many states the total amount paid from any one bond to nonowner claimants cannot exceed certain amounts. For example, if a general contractor has a $10,000 bond, $8,000 of that bond may be reserved for the owner of the improvement.

If there exists three subcontractors who, together, have supplied $6,000 worth of performance on a project, the general contractors bond could only offer $2,000 worth of compensation to be divided among the three subcontractors.

In many states, companies are forming to provide "pre-claim notices," or right to lien notices for suppliers, subcontractors, and others who provide labor and material.

Priority

In most cases, recovery from the general contractor's surety bond is on a first-come, first-served basis, noting the above limitations on payment amounts. However, on a $2,000 bond, an owner will receive priority over nonowner claimants, providing the owner has filed a claim within the time frame specified by statute.

Determinations and judgments as a result of claims against a contractor by the owner of a residential structure often have payment priority to the full extent of the bond over all other types of claims.

Tip

For further details regarding priority issues and judgments on bonds, consult with your contractor's bonding company or your insurance agency.

Claims with the Licensing or Registration Agencies

Some states, where contractors are licensed or registered, have departments in the agency that process claims and take action against licensed or registered contractors and subcontractors who get into a dispute with residential owners. Filing a claim with this agency may be another means to securing payment for performance on a construction project without filing a lien.

The agency is usually authorized to charge a deposit for filing a claim, requesting a hearing, or filing exceptions. The deposit may be refunded if the party attends the proceedings, or may be used as a fee for hearing expenses as the agency has it set up.

Warning

In most states, the construction contractor has to be licensed or registered at the time the contract was entered into, and during the time the work was performed. An unlicensed or unregistered contractor, making contracts or performing work, may not ordinarily be able to file a claim, file a lien, or sue for construction contract performance with the agency or with a court.

Acceptable Claims

Different states and agencies may use a combination of mediation and arbitration to settle claims. The licensing or registration agency will accept and make determinations on claims filed by owners against licensed or registered contractors that involve contracts for work on the following types of projects:

- Residential structures or appurtenances when the total contract or dispute amount is below certain minimum amounts
- Nonresidential property when the total contract amount is below certain minimum amounts
- A ground area of 4,000 square feet or less, or some other maximum
- Height from the top surface is 20 feet or less from the lowest flooring to the highest interior overhead finish of the building, or two story residential structure

Most licensing or registration agencies will only accept and make determinations on the following types of claims:

- Claims by the owner against the general contractor for:

  ◆ Negligent work

Sometimes a person will start a dispute because they want an advantage. They will not state this, but it can become apparent. When this is the case, your contract and lien law can be useful.

- Improper work
- Breach of contract

■ Claims by the owner against the general contractor to recoup money spent to release a lien
■ Claims by a licensed or registered general contractor against a licensed or registered subcontractor for:

- Negligent work
- Improper work
- Breach of contract

■ Claims by a person furnishing labor to a contractor.
■ Claims by persons furnishing material or renting supplies to a contractor.

Unacceptable Claims

Contractors and suppliers in public and nonqualifying commercial construction projects are not covered through most agencies claim's processes. On these types of projects protection against nonpayment is accomplished through special surety bonds known as *performance bonds*. Contractors on a public or commercial construction project normally have to post a performance bond, cashier's check, or certified check equal to the contract price of the project for faithful performance of the contract.

Suits against performance bonds normally require court action and are not handled by the licensing or registration agency. Remember, public projects are never subject to lien law resolution processes.

Note
The licensing or registration agency may refuse to accept a claim, or discontinue processing a claim, if the claim has also been submitted to a court or any other entity authorized by the law or disputing parties to be resolved. This action results in only one settlement process going on at one time.

Claims Process

The "Statement of Claim" form is used to begin the residential claims process. If the claim is accepted, a process with up to six steps would follow.

Giving someone a chance to vent anger or frustration will not settle a dispute. There has to be a new position for both parties, not just a way to be upset about the other parties position.

Investigation: If the licensing or registration agency accepts a filed claim, it will begin an investigation. Usually this means that an investigator from the claims division of the licensing or registration agency will visit the work site with the disputing parties present.

The investigator will listen to each party's argument. This may include written documentation as well as verbal statements from the disputing parties.

Mediation: The investigator then acts as a mediator and tries to develop a settlement that is agreeable to both parties. The investigator will recommend a settlement that is consistent with the terms of the contract and represents accepted standards of workmanship and trade practices.

Litigation can take years. Arbitration can take months, mediation can be done in a matter of weeks.

Arbitration: If the disputing parties are unable to reach a settlement, the case will be arbitrated by the investigator. In an arbitration, the investigator reviews the evidence in each case and then issues an order. The order will call for a specific action and may dismiss the case or require a specific action from the contractor.

Hearing: If either party objects to the arbitrated settlement, the next step is to request an administrative hearing.

An arbitration clause in a contract will routinely be enforced by a court as a mutually agreed way to settle a dispute. If you have an arbitration clause in your contract, be sure you know how it works and how it would work for you in a dispute.

An Administrative Law Judge or hearings officer would determine if the claim is valid and the dollar amount of the claim.

The Administrative Law Judge or hearings officer will reach a conclusion after reviewing the testimony, evidence, and witnesses produced by disputing parties. The burden of proof is upon the parties presenting their case. The case with the most persuasive evidence normally wins.

Note
    Parties may normally bring their attorneys.

Final Order: The final order is issued by the administrator of the

The common approach to dispute resolution is to make the other person understand your view. The idea is that this will make the dispute go away. The problem is the other person knows your view and rejects it. More explanation just secures the disputed issue.

agency after a hearing, or the claims appeal committee after an exception hearing. Final orders for claims become final shortly after they are issued if no exceptions are filed.

The contractor may have 30 days in which to comply with the final order or file a request for stay with the agency.

Exception Hearing: Either party may be able to contest the ruling of the Administrative Law Judge or hearings officer by filing a written exception with the licensing or registration Claims Appeal Committee. The Appeal Committee would meet to hear the testimony and final arguments of the parties. After reviewing each case, the Appeal Committee will issue a final order.

Appeal: Either party might be able to challenge the final order ruling by filing an appeal with the state court of appeals.

Note
No new testimony is allowed at this appeal hearing.

Alternative Dispute Resolution

As a construction contractor and business person, you should always opt to secure payment for performance and resolve disputes. Alternative dispute resolution allows you to do both and could be a practical alternative to lien action.

You can keep disputes at bay by teaching your staff about dispute management. Make it a company policy to immediately resolve disputes. Give your staff the authority to make decisions about a dispute, and note those areas where they do not have authority to do so. Get your staff familiar with that noted area, and train them to help the customer get to the correct person to resolve the issue.

Alternative means of dispute resolution include:

- Negotiation
- Mediation
- Med-Arb (combination of mediation and arbitration)
- Arbitration

There are organizations that have established rules under which trained mediators and arbitrators operate. Many of the mediators and arbitrators are judges and lawyers who you can hire at a modest cost.

Tip
Because of the complexity of construction contract cases, you would be wise to mediate or arbitrate according to the rules of an organization experienced in settling construction contract disputes. Two such organizations are the:

- American Arbitration Association
- Construction Arbitration Services

In a dispute, rely on expert information. Stay on course with reference to the contract and the details of other points relating to products and installation.

American Arbitration Association

The American Arbitration Association (AAA) is a private dispute resolution organization that acts as a clearinghouse for mediators and arbitrators who settle commercial, labor, and public sector disputes through:

- Arbitration
- Mediation
- Democratic election
- Other voluntary methods

The AAA establishes and maintains a group of individuals as members of the Construction Industry Panel of Arbitrators who are qualified to arbitrate because of their current experience in the construction field.

The AAA itself does not mediate or arbitrate settlements but supplies disputing parties with lists of arbitrators or mediators for their mutual selection.

Tip
If you believe that mediation or arbitration are workable alternatives to litigation, include a mediation or arbitration clause in your contract. Adding an arbitration clause to the contract will expedite a settlement in a dispute.

You can also settle an existing dispute through mediation or arbitration by adding the appropriate AAA clause to the contract, providing all parties to the contract are in agreement.

Your contract should contain the dispute prevention method you desire. It is part of your contractor work to sell the customer on the idea of using this means to settle a dispute.

For more information about American Arbitration Association services, write to:

American Arbitration Association
811 First Avenue, Suite 200
Seattle, Washington 98104-1455
Telephone Number: (206) 622-6435
Fax Number: (206) 343-5679

Construction Arbitration Services

Construction Arbitration Services (CAS) is a private, independent, impartial organization which administers dispute resolution procedures focused on the construction industry. These procedures include:

- Home Owners Warranty (HOW)
- Home Buyers Warranty 210
- Arbitration

If contractual parties would like to settle a dispute by arbitration according to CAS rules, include the appropriate clause in the contract.

For more information about Construction Arbitration Services, write:

Construction Arbitration Services
2777 Stemmons Freeway #650
Dallas, Texas 75207
Telephone Number: (214) 638-2700
FAX Number: (214) 638-4054

According to AAA, more than 85% of disputes that are mediated are settled.

Summary

Congratulations! You have just completed the *Advantage Contractor Business Success Series* course on lien law and other related issues.

The subject of lien law is technical in nature as are the requirements for perfecting, and foreclosing a claim of lien. If you are unsure about any part of the lien process, obtain the services of a competent attorney.

Quick Reference Tool

Abandonment

The act of abandoning means to cease to assert or exercise an interest, right or title to something. In the context of the construction project, a project is considered abandoned on the 75th day after work on construction of the improvement ceases, or when the owner, mortgagee of the improvement, or the agent of either one posts and records a "Notice of Abandonment."

Agency

The relationship between a principal and his or her agent is called agency. The agent has certain powers of the principal which are granted by the principal to the agent.

Agent

An agent is a person authorized by another to act on his or her behalf.

Arbitration

Arbitration is the hearing and determination of a dispute between parties by a person or persons (arbitrators) chosen or agreed to by the parties. The decision of the arbitrator is binding to the disputing parties.

Assignment

An assignment is a transfer of a legal right by one party to another party.

Attach

In a legal context, to attach means to take persons or property by legal authority.

Breach

To breach a contract is to break a promise. A contractual party is said to be in breach of contract when that party fails to fulfill the obligations assigned by the terms and conditions under the contract. There are degrees of breach: material and nonmaterial.

- Material breach is serious deviation from the performance of promises under the contract. This could include using items greatly outside the specifications, or abandoning the project.

- Nonmaterial breach is one that does not affect the nature of the project. This could include using an item in the project of a similar type specified in the contract, or not completing the project by the time specified in the contract.

Charge

A charge used in a legal context is a monetary burden, encumbrance, tax, lien, expense, or liability to pay.

Claimant

A claimant is a person who declares and demands the recognition of a right, title, possession, etc.

Competency

Someone with competency has legal capacity or qualification based on minimum requirements, such as age, soundness of mind, or citizenship.

Contractual Right

A contractual right is a right to performance that is granted to parties as a result of their signed agreement.

Damages

Damages are losses caused to one party of the contract as a result of breach by the other party. Damages are awarded by the court and are intended as remedies to compensate someone who has not received what he or she bargained for.

Debt

A debt is something that one person is obligated to pay or to perform for another.

Defer

To defer is to postpone something until a future date with the intention of beginning or resuming it then.

Encumbrance

An encumbrance is a burden or claim on property, such as a mortgage, a lien, or a judgment. Claiming a lien places an encumbrance on the land or improvement of another.

Enforceable Contract

An enforceable contract is one that is valid and has clear intent and understandable terms and conditions.

Estoppel

Estoppel is a rule of law that stops someone from being able to deny an existing legal obligation.

Execute

Execute, used in a legal context, means to carry through to completion in the manner prescribed, or to give validity to a legal instrument by fulfilling the legal requirements of it. For example, conforming to the terms and conditions in completing a signed contract.

Extent

The extent of something is the space or degree to which a thing reaches; for example, the length, area, volume or scope.

File (a lien)

To file a lien is to record a "Claim of Lien" with the recording clerk in the county where the property is located.

Foreclose

To foreclose is to take away the right to redeem. For example, a mortgagor (recorded security interest holder of a property) would be deprived of the right to redeem his or her property because of failure to make mortgage payments when due.

Foreclosure

Foreclosure, used in the context of lien law, is taking possession of a property in which there is a specific claim. The act of recovering the lienable dollar amount of a claim.

Improvement

A building or structure constructed on real property that increases the value of that property.

Insolvent

To be insolvent is to be unable to satisfy creditors or pay money owed (debt) because the debt is greater than the assets (cash or items that can be exchanged for cash) or because of an inability to pay debts as they mature. Bankrupt.

Judgment

A recording with the county indicating an encumbrance to a parcel of real property. Judgments are normally a result of liens, suits, or debts.

Lienable Performance

Lienable performance, used in the context of lien law, refers to a person's eligibility to perfect a lien based on the nature of the work provided in the improvement of residential property. Lienable performance defined under the statutes includes:

- Materials furnished for an improvement
- Transportation of materials
- Equipment rental
- Contribution to an employee benefit fund
- Plans, drawings, specifications, and supervision
- Site preparation or development

Litigation

Bringing a lawsuit to court; taking legal action.

Material Breach

An action or lack of action that significantly upsets the intent of the agreement and changes the essence of the contract.

Materialman

A materialman is a term formerly used in the statutes to designate the supplier of materials on a construction project.

Materialmen's Lien

A materialmen's lien is a term formerly used in the statutes to indicate the legal right to hold property or to have it sold or applied for payment of a claim. This legal right is granted by the statutes to persons who provide labor, materials, or certain services that are incorporated into, consumed in, or contribute to the improvement of privately owned real property.

Mechanic's Lien

A mechanic's lien is a term formerly used in the statutes to indicate the legal right to hold property or to have it sold or applied for payment of a claim. This legal right is granted by the statutes to persons who provide labor, materials, or certain services that are incorporated into, consumed in, or contribute to the improvement of privately-owned real property.

Nonmaterial Breach

An action or lack of action that does not significantly upset the intent of the agreement or change the essence of the contract.

Overhead Expense

An overhead expense pertains to the general cost of running a business.

Perfect a Lien

To record the lien with the recording clerk in the county where the property is located. At this point in time a lien is actually created.

Performance

Completing the terms and specifications required in a contract. Performance may be partial (a specific part of the contract), or complete (fulfilling all terms of the contract).

Promissory Note

A promissory note is a written promise to pay a specified sum of money to a designated person, to his or her order, or to the bearer of the note at a fixed time or on demand.

Quasi Contract

A quasi contract is not really a contract because one or more essential elements are missing. However, the courts sometimes will apply a remedial judgment to prevent *unjust enrichment* of another.

Real Property

Real property is distinguished from personal property and refers to an estate or property consisting of all lands and of all appurtenances to lands, such as buildings, crops, or mineral rights.

Reasonable Certainty

Reasonable certainty, used in the context of law, pertains to issues of compensation. For example, the value attached to any work performed or materials supplied must be proven to be a logical fact.

Recovery

Recovery, used in the context of law, means to obtain the right to something by verdict or judgment of a court of law.

Secure

Secure, used in the context of a financial transaction, means to assure a creditor of payment by the pledge or mortgaging of property.

Special Damages

Special damages are awarded in addition to *damages*. These special damages are compensation for losses that occurred as a result of a "chain reaction" stemming from the original breach. For example, a homeowner could be awarded special damages for costs incurred in renting a motel room because of a leak in the roof for which the contractor is liable.

Statute

A statute is an order or ruling made by the legislature and expressed in a formal document. The statutes that pertain to the construction industry are contained in your state laws and are cross-referenced where necessary to cover other cases, as in construction liens.

Statutory

Something that is statutory is prescribed or authorized by statute.

Statutory Agent

In many states, a statutory agent is called a "construction agent." The construction agent includes the contractor, architect, builder, lessee, vendee, or any other person having charge of any improvement to real property.

Subcontractor

A contractor who contracts with the general (primary) contractor or with another subcontractor, but not directly with the owner. The subcontractor is responsible for specific portions of the project and is subject to the terms and conditions of the primary contract.

Substantial Completion

Substantial completion refers to that point in a particular project when the majority of the work has been completed.

Final payment, contract enforcement, and the right to lien are contingent upon a definition of complete performance.

Surety Bond

A surety bond is security against loss or damage or the fulfillment of an obligation. To register, the state requires construction contractors to obtain a surety bond that will pay for any claims arising out of:

- Improper work
- Breach of contract
- Failure to pay persons performing labor or furnishing material or equipment for construction

Unenforceable Contract

An unenforceable contract cannot be enforced in a court of law because it does not meet statutory requirements or lacks clear, understandable terms and/or intent.

Unjust Enrichment

Unjust enrichment, used in the context of law, refers to a situation where one party prospers unjustly at the expense of another. To prevent this from happening, the courts may enforce a quasi contract.

For example, a homeowner may be required to pay the contractor for the deck built even though a valid contract did not exist. The homeowner would be unjustly enriched if he was permitted to keep the deck at the total expense of the contractor.

Valid

Something that is valid has legal force and is supportable in law.

Valid Contract

A valid contract includes the following four essential elements:

- Offer and acceptance
- Consideration
- Competent parties (legal capacity)
- Legal purpose

In addition, the contract must be in written form if required by statute.

Valid Lien

A valid lien is a well-founded claim that is supportable in law.

Voidable

This term refers to a concept of contract law. A contract is voidable when one party to the contract has the option of not allowing the other party to enforce the contract. If a contractor makes a construction contract while not registered, the contract is voidable. The contractor has lost all rights of enforcement while the owner has an option to enforce or not enforce the contract.

Waive

To waive, in the context of law, is to intentionally relinquish a known right or interest.

Waiver

A waiver is a voluntary surrender of a legal right, for example, the right to lien. A right may be waived by including a specific clause in the contract, by signing a completed waiver form, or it may be presumed by one's actions or lack of actions.

You, Our Customer

As our customer, we are happy to demonstrate our customer service to you. As with all our courses, we at the Academy offer our services to you through these courses. If you have questions or problems, we would be happy to talk to you.

We ask that you follow this process:

1. Read the course and check out the Bibliography for more leads on your question. If you have a library available, you can check out the books or ask the librarian how to find them. Please check at least one resource before contacting us.

2. Frame your question(s) on paper before contacting us. You will find it very useful to write your question down. In this way you make sure you know exactly what you want to ask.

3. Our first response to your question will usually be to refer you to other courses in the Advantage Contractor Business Success Series, or Resources in the courses. We want you to learn how to find information on your own. Developing skill at finding information gives you a powerful advantage as a contractor. If you rely on us for your information, you are limited and become dependent on us. Remember, you are an **independent** construction contractor.

4. If, after looking for information on your own, you still have a question, please contact us. We assume at this point that your question will now be more detailed, having gathered some information. However, we may still refer you to a specific source which will answer your question. The object of this process will be similar to what a teacher would do in assisting you to learn how to ask informed questions and find new sources of answers.

How to contact us in order of our preference:

A. E-Mail: Info@Contracting-Academy.com
B. Fax inquiry: 541-344-5387
C. US Mail: 83 Centennial Loop, Eugene, OR 97401
D. Phone: 541-344-1442

Thanks for your cooperation in following this process.

State Offices That Provide Small Business Help

Alabama
Alabama Development Office
State Capitol
Montgomery, AL 36130
(800) 248-0333* (205) 263-0048

Alaska
Division of Economic Development
Department of Commerce and Economic
    Development
PO Box D
Juneau, AK 99811
(907) 465-2017

Arizona
Office of Business Finance
Department of Commerce
3800 North Central Avenue
Suite 1500
Phoenix, AZ 85012
(602) 280-1341

Arkansas
Small Business Information Center
Industrial Development Commission
State Capitol Mall
Room 4C-300
Little Rock, AR 72201
(501) 682-5275

California
Office of Small Business
Department of Commerce
801 K Street, Suite 1700
Sacramento, CA 95814
(916) 327-4357 (916) 445-6545

Colorado
One-Stop Assistance Center
1560 Broadway, Suite 1530
Denver, CO 80202
(800) 333-7798 (303) 592-5920

Connecticut
Small Business Services
Department of Economic Development
865 Brook Street
Rocky Hill, CN 06067
(203) 258-4269

Delaware
Development Office
PO Box 1401
99 Kings Highway
Dover, DE 19903
(302) 736-4271

District of Columbia
Office of Business and Economic
    Development
Tenth Floor
717 14th Street NW
Washington, DC 20005
(202) 727-6600

Florida
Bureau of Business Assistance
Department of Commerce
107 West Gaines Street, Room 443
Tallahassee, FL 32399-2000
(800) 342-0771*

* In state calling only

Georgia

Department of Community Affairs
100 Peachtree Street, Suite 1200
Atlanta, GA 30303
(404) 656-6200

Hawaii

Small Business Information Service
737 Bishop Street, Suite 1900
Honolulu, HI 96813
(808) 578-7645 (808) 543-6691

Idaho

Economic Development Division
Department of Commerce
700 State Street
Boise, ID 83720-2700
(208) 334-2470

Illinois

Small Business Assistance Bureau
Department of Commerce and
    Community Affairs
620 East Adams Street
Springfield, IL 62701
(800) 252-2923*

Indiana

Ombudsman's Office
Business Development Division
Department of Commerce
One North Capitol, Suite 700
Indianapolis, IN 46204-2288
(800) 824-2476* (317) 232-7304

Iowa

Bureau of Small Business Development
Department of Economic Development
200 East Grand Avenue
Des Moines, IA 50309
(800) 532-1216* (515) 242-4899

Kansas

Division of Existing Industry
Development
400 SW Eighth Street
Topeka, KS 66603
(785) 296-5298

Kentucky

Division of Small Business
Capitol Plaza Tower
Frankfort, KY 40601
(800) 626-2250* (502) 564-4252

Louisiana

Development Division
Office of Commerce and Industry
PO Box 94185
Baton Rouge, LA 70804-9185
(504) 342-5365

Maine

Business Development Division
State Development Office
State House
Augusta, ME 04333
(800) 872-3838* (207) 289-3153

Maryland

Division of Business Development
Department of Economic and
Employment Development
217 East Redwood Street
Baltimore, MD 21202
(800) 873-7232 (301) 333-6996

Massachusetts

Office of Business Development
100 Cambridge Street
13th Floor
Boston, MA 02202
(617) 727-3206

* In state calling only

Michigan

Michigan Business Ombudsman
Department of Commerce
PO Box 30107
Lansing, MI 48909
(800) 232-2727* (517) 373-6241

Minnesota

Small Business Assistance Office
Department of Trade and Economic
Development
900 American Center Building
150 East Kellogg Boulevard
St. Paul, MN 55101
(800) 652-9747 (612) 296-3871

Mississippi

Small Business Bureau
Research and Development Center
PO Box 849
Jackson, MS 39205
(601) 359-3552

Missouri

Small Business Bureau
Research and Development Center
PO Box 118
Jefferson City, MO 65102
(314) 751-4982 (314) 751-8411

Montana

Business Assistance Division
Department of Commerce
1424 Ninth Ave.
Helena, MT 59620
(800) 221-8015* (406) 444-2801

Nebraska

Existing Business Division
Department of Economic Development
PO Box 94666
301 Centennial Mall South
Lincoln, NE 68509-4666
(402) 471-3782

Nevada

Nevada Commission of Economic
Development
Capitol Complex
Carson City, NV 89710
(702) 687-4325

New Hampshire

Small Business Development Center
University Center
400 Commercial Street, Room 311
Manchester, NH 03101
(603) 625-4522

New Jersey

Office of Small Business Assistance
Department of Commerce and Economic
Development
20 West State Street, CN 835
Trenton, NJ 08625
(609) 984-4442

New Mexico

Economic Development Division
Department of Economic Development
1100 St. Francis Drive
Santa Fe, NM 87503
(505) 827-0300

New York

Division for Small Business
Department of Economic Development
1515 Broadway
51st Floor
New York, NY 10036
(212) 827-6150

North Carolina

Small Business Development Division
Department of Economic and
Community Development
Dobbs Building, Room 2019
430 North Salisbury Street
Raleigh, NC 27611
(919) 733-2810

* In state calling only

North Dakota

Small Business Coordinator
Economic Development Commission
Liberty Memorial Building
604 East Boulevard
Bismark, ND 58505
(701) 224-2810

Ohio

Small and Developing Business Division
Department of Development
PO Box 1001
Columbus, OH 43266-0101
(800) 248-4040* (614) 466-4232

Oklahoma

Oklahoma Department of Commerce
PO Box 26980
6601 N. Broadway Extension
Oklahoma City, OK 73126-0980
(800) 477-6552* (405) 843-9770

Oregon

Economic Development Department
775 Summer Street NE
Salem, OR 97310
(800) 233-3306* (503) 373-1200

Pennsylvania

Bureau of Small Business and
    Appalachian Development
Department of Commerce
461 Forum Building
Harrisburg, PA 17120
(717) 783-5700

Puerto Rico

Commonwealth Department of
    Commerce
Box S
4275 Old San Juan Station
San Juan, PR 00905
(809) 721-3290

Rhode Island

Business Development Division
Department of Economic Development
Seven Jackson Walkway
Providence, RI 02903
(401) 277-2601

South Carolina

Enterprise Development
PO Box 1149
Columbia, SC 29202
(800) 922-6684* (803) 737-0888

South Dakota

Governor's Office of Economic
    Development
Capital Lake Plaza
711 Wells Avenue
Pierre, SD 57501
(800) 872-6190* (605) 773-5032

Tennessee

Small Business Office
Department of Economic and
Community Development
320 Sixth Avenue North
Seventh Floor
Rachel Jackson Building
Nashville, TN 37219
(800) 872-7201* (615) 741-2626

Texas

Small Building Division
Department of Commerce
Economic Development Commission
PO Box 12728
Capitol Station
410 East Fifth Street
Austin, TX 78711
(800) 888-0511 (512) 472-5059

* In state calling only

Utah

Small Business Development Center
102 West 500 South, Suite 315
Salt Lake City, UT 84101
(801) 581-7905

Vermont

Agency of Development and Community
   Affairs
The Pavilion
109 State Street
Montpelier, VT 05609
(800) 622-4553* (802) 828-3221

Virginia

Small Business and Financial Services
Department of Economic Development
PO Box 798
1000 Washington Building
Richmond, VA 23206
(804) 371-8252

Washington

Small Business Development Center
245 Todd Hall
Washington State University
Pullman, WA 99164-4727
(509) 335-1576

West Virginia

Small Business Development Center
   Division
1115 Virginia Street East
Charleston, WV 25301
(304) 348-2960

Wisconsin

Public Information Bureau
Department of Development
PO Box 7970
123 West Washington Avenue
Madison, WI 53707
(800) 435-7287* (608) 266-1018

Wyoming

Economic Development and
Stabilization Board
Herschler Building
Cheyenne, WY 82002
(307) 777-7287

* In state calling only
Source: National Association for the Self-
Employed,
USA TODAY research

Resources

The following sources are generally recognized as associated members of the building industry that have impact on standards and guidelines of business operations. You can contact these sources to get specific information on products and business ideas in your specific trade or business area. In some cases you can go to a local chapter for help. These associations will be promoting their product or service, but will also be able to answer many business, technical and product questions.

Air Conditioning Contractors of America (ACCA)
1513 16th St. NW
Washington, DC 20036

Air Conditioning and Refrigeration Institute
4301 N. Fairfax Dr. Suite 425
Arlington, VA 22203
(703) 524-8800

Aluminum Association (AA)
900 19th St. NW, Ste. 300
Washington, DC 20006
(202) 862-5100

American Association of Nurserymen
1250 I St. NW, Suite 500
Washington, DC 20005
(202) 789-2900

American Building Contractors Assn.
PO Box 2772
Cypress, CA 90630
(714) 828-4760
http://www.netcom.com/~w-e/ abca.html

American Concrete Institute (ACI)
P.O. Box 19150
Detroit, MI 48219

American Gas Association
1515 Wilson Blvd.
Arlington, VA 22209
(703) 841-8589

American Hardboard Association
520 N. Hicks Rd.
Palatine, IL 60067
(312) 934-8800

American Hardware Manufacturers Association (AHMA)
801 N. Plaza Drive
Schaumburg, IL 60173-4977
(847) 605-1025

American Institute of Building Design
991 Post Rd. E.
Westport, CT 06880
(800) 366-2423

American Institute of Steel Construction, Inc.
1 E. Wacker Dr., Ste. 3100
Chicago, IL 60601-2001
(312) 670-2400

American Institute of Timber Construction (AITC)
11818 SE Mill Plain Blvd., Ste. 415
Vancouver, WA 98684
(206) 254-9132

American Insurance Association (AIA)

1130 Connecticut Ave. NW, Ste. 1000
Washington, DC 20036
(202) 828-7100

American Iron and Steel Institute (AISI)

1133 15th St. NW
Washington, DC 20005
(202) 452-7100

America Lighting Association

World Trade Center
PO Box 420288
Dallas, TX 75342-0288
(800) 605-4448

American National Standards Institute (ANSI)

11 W. 42nd St., 13th floor
New York, NY 10036
(212) 642-4900

American Plywood Association (APA)

P.O. Box 11700
Tacoma, WA 98411
(206) 565-6600

American Society of Heating, Refrigeration and Air Conditioning Engineers

1791 Tullie Circle NE
Atlanta, GA 30329
(404) 636-8400

American Society of Home Inspectors

85 W. Algonquin Rd., Suite 360
Arlington Heights, IL 60005
(800) 743-ASHI (2744)

American Society of Interior Designers

608 Massachusetts Ave. NW
Washington, DC 20002-6006
(202) 546-3480

American Society of Testing Materials (ASTM)

100 Bar Harbor Dr.
West Conshohocken, PA 19428-2959
(610) 832-9500

American Solar Energy Society (ASES)

2400 Central Ave. Suite G1
Boulder, CO 80301
(303) 443-3130

American Subcontractors Association

1004 Duke St.
Alexandria, VA 22314
(703) 684-3450
ASAoffice@aol.com

American Welding Society, Inc. (AWS)

550 LeJeune Rd. NW, P.O. Box 351040
Miami, FL 33135
(305) 443-9353

American Wood-Preservers Association (AWPA)

P.O. Box 286
Woodstock, MD 21163-0286
(410) 465-3169

American Wood Preservers Bureau (AWPB)

P.O. Box 5283
Springfield, VA 22150
(703)339-6660

American Wood Preservers Institute (AWPI)

1945 Old Gallows Rd., Ste. 550
Vienna, VA 22182

Appraisal Institute

875 N. Michigan Ave. Suite 2400
Chicago, IL 60611-1980
(312) 335-4100

Architectural Woodwork Institute
13924 Braddock Rd. Suite 100
Centreville, VA 22020-1910
(703) 222-1100

Asphalt Roofing Manufacturers
6288 Montrose Rd.
Rockville, MD 20852
(301) 231-9050

Association for Preservation Technology
PO Box 3511
Williamsburgh, VA 23187
(703) 373-1621

Association for Safe & Accessible Products
1511 K. St., N. W., Suite 600
Washington, OR 20005-4905
(202) 347-8200
asapdc@aol.com

Association of Construction Inspectors
8383 E. Evans St.
Scottsdale, AZ 85260
(602) 998-8021
aci@iami.org
http://iami.org/aci.html

Association of Home Appliance Manufacturers
20 N. Wacker Dr.
Chicago, IL 60606-2806
(312) 984-5800

Brick Institute of America (BIA)
11490 Commerce Park Dr.
Reston, VA 22091
(703) 620-0010

Building Systems Councils of NAHB
15th & M Streets NW
Washington, DC 20005

Canadian Home Builders' Association
150 Laurier Ave. W. Suite 200
Ottawa, ON K1P 5J4 Canada
(613) 230-3060

Canadian Retail Hardware Association (CRHA)
6800 Campobello Rd.
Mississauga, ON L5N 2L8 Canada
(905) 821-3470

The Carpet and Rug Institute
PO Box 2049
Dalton, GA 30722-2048
(706) 278-3176

Cast Iron Soil Pipe Institute
5939 Shallowford Rd. Suite 419
Chattanooga, TN 37421
615-892-0137

Cedar Shake and Shingle Bureau
515 116th Ave. NW, Ste. 275
Bellevue, WA 98004-5294
(206) 453-1323

Cellulose Insulation Manufacturers Association
136 S. Keowee St.
Dayton, OH 45402
(513) 222-2464
assocoffice@delphi.com
ah803@dayton.wright.edu

Ceramic Tile Institute of America
800 Roosevelt Rd. Bldg C, Suite 20
Glen Ellyn, IL 60137
(708) 545-9415

Concrete Reinforcing Steel Institute (CRSI)
933 Plum Grove Rd.
Schaumburg, IL 60173

Decorative Laminate Products Association
13924 Braddock Rd., Suite 100
Centreville, VA 22020
(800) 684-3572

Energy Efficiency and Renewable Energy Clearinghouse (EREC)
PO Box 3048
Merrifield, VA 22116
(800) 363-3732
doe.erec@nciinc.com
http://www.erecbbs.nciinc.com

The Environmental Information Assn.
4915 Auburn Ave., Suite 303
Bethesda, MD 20814
(301) 961-4999

Forest Products Research Society
2801 Marshall Court
Madison, WI 53705
(608) 231-1361

Garage Door Hardware Association
2850 S. Ocean Blvd., Suite 311
Palm Beach, FL 33480-5535
(407) 533-0991

Gypsum Association (GA)
810 1st St. NE, Suite 510
Washington, DC 20002
(202) 289-5440

Hardwood Plywood Manufacturer's Association (HPMA)
1825 Michael Faraday Dr., P.O. Box 2789
Reston, VA 22090

Home Automation Association
808 17th St. NW, Suite 200
Washington, DC 20006-3910
(202) 223-9669
75250.1274@copuserve.com

Home Fashion Products Association
355 Lexington Ave. 17th Fl.
New York, NY 10017-6603

Home Improvement Research Institute
400 Knightsbridge Pkwy
Lincolnshire, IL 60069-3646
847-634-4368

Home Inspection Institute of America
314 Main St.
PO Box 4174
Yalesville Wallingford, CT 06492
(203) 284-2311
homeinspi@aol.com

Home Ventilating Institute
30 W. University Dr.
Arlington Heights, IL 60004-1806
(708) 394-0150

International Masonry Institute
823 15th St. NW
Washington, DC 20005
(202) 783-3908

International Wood Products Assn.
4214 Kings St. W.
Alexandria, VA 22302
(703) 820-6696
info@ihpa.org
http//www.ihpa.org

Italian Tile Association
305 Madison Ave., Suite 3120
New York, NY 10165-0111
(212) 661-0435

Kitchen Cabinet Manufacturers Association
1899 Preston White Dr.
Reston, VA 22091
(703) 264-1690

Manufactured Housing Institute
1745 Jefferson Davis Hwy., Ste. 511
Arlington, VA 22202

Maple Flooring Manufacturers Association
60 Revere Dr., Suite 500
Northbrook, IL 60062
(708) 480-9138

Mechanical Contractors Association of America
1385 Piccard Dr.
Rockville, MD 20850
(301) 869-5800

Metal Building Manufacturers Association (MBMA)
2130 Keith Building
Cleveland, OH 44115

Metal Lath/Steel Framing Association Division
600 5. Federal St., Ste. 400
Chicago, IL 60605
(312) 922-6222

Mineral Insulation Manufacturers Association
1420 King St.
Alexandria, VA 22314

National Assn. of Brick Distributors
1600 Spring Hill Rd., Suite 305
Vienna, VA 22182
(703) 749-6223

National Association of Electrical Distributors
45 Danbury Rd.
Wilton, CT 06897
(203) 834-1908

National Association of Home Builders (NAHB)
1201 15th St., NW
Washington, DC 20005-2800
(202) 822-0200

National Association of Home Builders Remodelers Council
1201 15th St., N. W.
Washington, DC 20005-2800
(800) 368-5242 Ext. 216

National Association of Home Inspectors
4248 Park Glen Rd.
Minneapolis, MN 55416
(800) 448-3942
assnhdqs@usinternet.com

National Association of Plumbing-Heating-Cooling Contractors
PO Box 6808
Falls Church, VA 22040
(800) 533-7694
naphcc@naphcc.org
http://www.naphcc.org

National Association of Real Estate Appraisers
8383 E. Evans Rd.
Scottsdale, AZ 85260
(602) 948-8000

National Association of the Remodeling Industry (NARI)
4900 Seminary Rd., Suite 320
Alexandria, VA 22311
(800) 966-7601

National Association of Women in Construction
327 S. Adams St.
Fort Worth, TX 76104-1002
(800) 552-3506

National Concrete Masonry Association (NCMA)
2302 Horse Pen Rd.
Herndon, VA 22071-3499
(703) 713-1900

National Decorating Products Association (NDPA)
1050 N. Lindbergh Blvd.
St. Louis, MO 63132-2994
(314) 991-3470

National Fire Protection Association (NFPA)
1 Batterymarch Park, P.O. Box 9101
Quincy, MA 02269-9101
(617) 770-3000

National Fire Sprinkler Association
Robin Hill Corp. Pk., Rt. 22, Box 1
Patterson, NY 12563
(617) 770-3000

National Forest Products Association
1250 Connecticut Ave. NW, Ste. 200
Washington, DC 20036
(202) 463-2700

National Kitchen and Bath Association (NKBA)
687 Willow Grove St.
Hackettstown, NJ 07840
(908) 852-0033

National Lime Association (MA)
3601 N. Fairfax Dr.
Arlington, VA 22201
(703) 243-5463

National Oak Flooring Manufacturers Association
PO Box 3009
Memphis, TN 38173
(901) 526-5016

National Particleboard Association (NPA)
18928 Premiere Ct.
Gaithersburg, MD 20879-1569
(301) 670-0604

National Pest Control Association (NPCA)
8100 Oak St.
Dunn Loring, VA 22027
(703) 573-8330

National Retail Hardware Assn.
5822 W. 74th St.
Indianapolis, IN 46278-1787
(317) 290-0338

National Roofing Contractors Association
10255 W. Higgins Rd., Suite 600
Rosemont, IL 60018
(800) 323-9545

National Spa and Pool Institute
2111 Eisenhower Ave.
Alexandria, VA 22314-4698
(703) 838-0083
http://www.resourcecenter.com

National Terrazzo and Mosaic Assn.
3166 Des Plaines Ave., Suite 121
Des Plaines, IL 60018-4223
(800) 323-9736

National Wood Flooring Assn.
233 Old Meremac Station Rd.
Manchester, MO 63021
(314)391-5161

National Wood Window and Door Assn.

1400 E. Touhy Ave., Suite 470
Des Plaines, IL 60018-3305
(800) 233-2301
nwwda@ais.net
http://www.nwwda.org

Noise Control Association

680 Rainier Ln.
Port Ludlow, WA 98365
(360) 437-0814

Northern American Insulation Manufacturers

44 Canal Center Plaza, Suite 310
Alexandria, VA 22314
(703) 684-0084

Oak Flooring Institute/National Oak Flooring Manufacturers Association

PO Box 3009
Memphis, TN 38173-0009
(901) 526-5016

Painting and Decorating Contractors of America (PDCA)

3913 Old Lee Hwy. #33-B
Fairfax, VA 22030
(800) 332-PDCA.

Portland Cement Association (PCA)

5420 Old Orchard Road
Skokie, IL 60077
(708) 966-6200

Resilient Floor Covering Institute

966 Hungerford Dr., Suite 12-B
Rockville, MD 20850-1714
(301) 340-8580

Roofing Industry Education Institute

14 Inverness Dr., Suite H-110
Englewood, CO 80112-5625
(303) 790-7200

Safe Building Alliance

655 15th St., N. W., Suite 1200
Washington, DC 20005-5701
(202) 879-5120

Sealed Insulating Glass Manufacturers Association

401 N. Michigan Ave.
Chicago, IL 60611-4212
(312) 644-6610
sigma@sba.com

Sheet Metal and Air Conditioning Contractor's National Association

P.O. Box 70
Merrifield, VA 22116
703-790-9890

Society of Certified Kitchen Designers

687 Willow Grove St.
Hackettstown, NJ 07840
(800) 843-6522

Society of the Plastics Industry (SPI) Spray Polyurethane Foam Division

1801 K. St., N. W., Suite 600K
Washington, DC 20006-1031
(800) 523-6154

Solar Energy Industries Association

122 C St., N. W., Fourth Floor
Washington, DC 20001
(202) 383-2600

Solar Rating and Certification Corp.

122 C St., N. W., Fourth Floor
Washington, DC 20001
(202) 383-2650

Southern Forest Products Association (SFPA)
> P.O. Box 641770
> Kenner, LA 70064-1700
> (504) 443-4464
> http://www.southernpine.com

Southern Pine Council
> PO Box 641770
> Kenner, LA 70064-1700
> (504) 443-4464
> http://www.southernpine.com

Southwest Research & Information Center (SRI)
> P.O. Box 4524
> Albuquerque, NM 87106
> 505-262-1862

Steel Joist Institute (SJI)
> 1205 48th Ave. N., Ste. A
> Myrtle Beach, SC 29577

Steel Window Institute (SWI)
> c/o Thomas Assocs., Inc.
> 2130 Keith Building
> Cleveland, OH 44115

Tile Contractors Assn. of America
> 11501 Georgia Ave., Suite 203
> Wheaton, MD 20902
> (800) OKK-TILE (655-8458)

Tile Council of America (TCA)
> P.O. Box 1787
> Clemson, SC 29633-1787
> (864) 646-TILE (8453)

Truss Plate Institute (TPI)
> 583 D'Onofrio Dr., Ste. 200
> Madison, WI 53719
> 608-833-5900

Underwriters' Laboratories (UL)
> 333 Pfingsten Road
> Northbrook, IL 60062

United American Contractors Assn.
> 85 Central St.
> Boston, MA 02109
> (617) 357-4470

Vinyl Siding Institute Div. of the Society of the Plastics Industry
> 1275 K. St., N. W., Suite 400
> Washington, DC 20005
> (202) 371-5200

Vinyl Window & Door Institute Div. of the Society of the Plastics Industry
> 1275 K. St., N. W., Suite 400
> Washington, DC 20005
> (202) 371-5200

Western Red Cedar Lumber Association
> 1100-555 Burrard St.
> Vancouver, BC V7x 1S7
> Canada
> (604) 684-0266
> wrcla@cofiho.cofi.org
> http://www.cofi.org/WRCLA

Western Wood Products Association (WWPA)
> Yeon Building, 522 SW 5th Ave., Suite 400
> Portland, OR 97204-2122
> 503-224-3930

Women Construction Owners & Executives, USA
> 4849 Connecticut Ave., N. W., Suite 706
> Washington, DC 20008-5838
> (800) 788-3548
> wcoeusa@aol.com

Bibliography

Lien and Bond Claims in the 50 States
Foundation of the American Subcontractors Association
(703) 684-3450

Canada Lien Law - Construction, Builder's and Mechanic's Lien in Canada
Macklem and Bristow, Thompson Professional Publications

Construction Contracts and Claims
Simon, Wily

Construction Forms and Contracts
Savage, Craftsman

Construction Law Principles and Practice
Jervis, McGraw-Hill

Contractor's Legal Kit
Ransome, Craftsman

Getting to Yes
Fisher, Penguin

Mechanics and Construction Liens in Alaska, Oregon, and Washington
Blum, Butterworth

Web Sites

These web site addresses have information about the topics covered in this course. You will have to look around the site for the information you need. You can benefit from using e-mail to contact people at the site about your questions. In addition, there are usually links to other sites that may be of interest.

If you are a veteran in using the internet, you already know that searching the internet can be frustrating and time consuming. Set out your questions on paper before you go to the internet. Then attempt to stick with these issues in your searching. Refrain from taking side trips until you have your questions answered.

Be sure to check our web site at:

www.Contracting-Academy.com

Building Tech Bookstore
http://www.BuildingTechBooks.com

Canadian Home Builders Association
http://www.buildermanual.com

http://www.magi.com/~homes/

Entreprenuer Magazine
http://www.entrepreurmag.com

Journal of Light Construction Builder's Forum
http://www.bginet.com/jlcforum/index.html

National Association of the Remodeling Industry
http://www.nari.org

National Association of Women in Construction
http://www.nawic@onramp.net (e-mail address)

Northwest Build Net
http://www.nwbuildnet.com

Lien Software
http://www.aecinfo.com/forum/soft

State by State Information
http://www.kwik-net.com/lien-st.html

Women Construction Owners and Executives
http://www.wcoeusa@aol.com (e-mail address)

http://www.abuildnet.com

http://www.build.com

http://www.builderbooksite.com

http://www.BuildingOnLine.com

http://www.carswell.com/cgi.bin/carswell

http://www.edgeonline.com

http://www.isquare.com

http://www.smartbiz.com

Remodeling Related

http://www.longrun.onweb.com/remodellinks.html

http://www.probuilder.com/home/home.html

http://www.builderweb.com

Search your favorite search engine using "Mechanic's Lien Law"

Web sites are constantly changing. These sites may change or even disappear. Those sites that are operated by contracting organizations are likely to be the most stable. Your search could lead to other new sites. Let us know if you find a good one.

Index

Date Due

BRODART, CO.   Cat. No. 23-233-003   Printed in U.S.A.